Hampton Court, Richmond and Kew Step by Step

By the same author

London Step by Step
Outer London Step by Step
Windsor and Eton Step by Step
London Churches Step by Step
Greenwich and East London Step by Step

Hampton Court, Richmond and Kew Step by Step

CHRISTOPHER TURNER

faber and faber
LONDON · BOSTON

First published in 1986
as part of *Outer London Step by Step*
by Faber and Faber Limited
3 Queen Square London WC1N 3AU
These sections first published
separately with revisions in 1987

Photoset by Parker Typesetting Service, Leicester
Printed in Great Britain by
Butler & Tanner Ltd Frome Somerset
All rights reserved

© Christopher Turner 1986, 1987
Drawings © Benoit Jacques 1986, 1987
Maps by Ken Smith

This book is sold subject to the condition that it shall not, by way of trade or otherwise, be lent, resold, hired out or otherwise circulated without the publisher's prior consent in any form of binding or cover other than that in which it is published and without a similar condition including this condition being imposed on the subsequent purchaser.

British Library Cataloguing in Publication Data

Turner, Christopher, *1934–*
Hampton Court, Richmond and Kew Step by Step.
1. Richmond upon Thames (London, England)
—Description—Guide-books
I. Title
914.21'9504858   DA690.R5
ISBN 0-571-14635-X

Contents

Acknowledgements viii
Introduction ix
Hampton Court 1
Richmond 19
Kew 35
Ham and Petersham 45
Twickenham 55

Acknowledgements

For their kindness and help I should like to thank the numerous librarians, architects, press officers, church officers, clerks, hoteliers and curators who have advised on and checked the contents of this book. A tremendous amount of valuable time was given by the following in particular: the London Tourist Board, the Historic Buildings and Monuments Commission, the Superintendent of Hampton Court and the Victoria and Albert Museum.

Introduction

Due to its historic buildings, great parks, sylvan riverside and easy communications with the capital's centre, the borough of Richmond-upon-Thames is regarded by many as outer London's most fortunate.

Its world famous sights are popular, not only with visitors, but with the Londoner as well. On the arrival of spring's first balmy weekend, the metropolitan resident thinks of the blossoms in Kew Gardens, the riverside at Richmond and the evocation of Tudor times at Hampton Court. All lie within the borough and may be reached by riverboat, as well as by road and rail.

Most of the information in this book has already appeared in *Outer London Step by Step* (Faber, 1986) but we believe that the Richmond area, because of its great popularity, also requires this separate volume, which will be partcularly appreciated by visitors to London with limited time at their disposal.

As with my other books in the *Step by Step* series, I have, throughout, attempted to put myself in the position of a complete stranger who, on arrival, wants to know *exactly* where to go and what route to follow.

Whether on a guided tour or a 'do it yourself' visit, *Hampton Court, Richmond and Kew Step by Step* will add immeasurably to your appreciation of this uniquely fascinating London borough. You will know what is open and when, you won't have to 'swot up' English history in advance and, above all, you won't get lost.

Christopher Turner

Hampton Court

The Tudor part of the palace, with its Great Hall, Chapel Royal and lofty chimney stacks, represents the finest royal building of its period to survive in England. It still evokes Henry VIII and his wives; five of the six lived here at some time. Of at least equal importance architecturally is the section designed by Sir Christopher Wren, which is, effectively, the greatest Baroque royal palace in the British Isles.

Timing Monday to Saturday is preferable, with an early morning start advisable. Allow at least half a day to see everything. The only interiors open throughout the year are the State Rooms, Renaissance Paintings Gallery and the 'Tudor' Tennis Court. The remainder generally close from October to March.

2 Hampton Court

Start *Hampton Court Station (BR) from Waterloo Station (BR). Exit and cross the bridge ahead. At the entrance to the second path R are the Trophy Gates.*

Alternatively, Hampton Court may be approached by river from Richmond Pier (30 minutes) or Westminster Pier (3 hours). If the tide is unfavourable the boat can take up to two hours longer from Richmond, so check first (940 2244). From Hampton Court Landing Stage turn L and continue to the first path R. This leads to the bridge over Hampton Court's moat (the Trophy Gates are seen later).

The main courtyards and grounds are open daily, 08.00–dusk. Admission free. Interiors are open April–September Monday–Saturday 09.30–18.00, Sunday 11.00–18.00. The State Rooms, Renaissance Paintings Gallery and 'Tudor' Tennis Court are also open October–March, Monday–Saturday 09.30–17.00, Sunday 14.00–17.00. Admission charge to the most important interiors.

Hampton Court Palace was first built in the Tudor period and then partially rebuilt almost two hundred years later. This is why it combines, unusually, both Tudor and Baroque styles. The western sections of the complex were commissioned by Thomas Wolsey as a manor house but soon extended by Henry VIII to become a royal palace. Adjoining this to the east are the state apartments built for William III and Mary II by *Wren*.

Wolsey, the son of an Ipswich butcher, was appointed Archbishop of York in 1515. In the same year he leased the manor of Hampton from the Knights of St John and the construction of Hampton Court began. The master mason was *John Lebons*. Within three years, Wolsey, now Henry VIII's favourite, had become Lord Chancellor, Cardinal and Papal Legate. He was the King's richest and most powerful subject and resided in a manor house more splendid than any of England's royal palaces.

Sensing Henry's envy, Wolsey fearfully assigned Hampton Court to the King in 1525, but was magnanimously allowed to remain in residence. In spite of tireless efforts, Wolsey failed to obtain the Pope's approval for Henry's divorce from Catherine of Aragon and for this failure was stripped of all his titles except that of Archbishop of York. He retired to York in 1530, but later that year Henry arrested him for high treason. Wolsey, however, was a sick man and died at Leicester on his way to London for trial and virtually certain execution.

Henry now occupied Hampton Court, carrying out major alterations between 1529 and 1538, and thereby creating the most sumptuous palace that England has ever known. It was the birthplace of his only son, later Edward VI.

During the Commonwealth, Hampton Court, together with its contents, remained relatively unscathed as it was appropriated by Oliver Cromwell for his personal use.

Following the accession of William and Mary in 1689, buildings to accommodate new royal apartments were designed, in the then current Classical style, by *Wren*. They replaced most of Henry VIII's State Apartments and it was planned to rebuild all of Hampton Court, except for the Great Hall, in similar style. This project was abandoned, however, and much of the old palace remains: England never did have its rival to Versailles.

Hampton Court

Many rooms in the palace were converted to 'grace and favour' homes in the 18C and they still serve this purpose.

The State Rooms were opened to the public by Queen Victoria in 1838.

| Location 1 | **TROPHY GATES** |

These were designed for William III, to provide the main entrance to the palace, but the trophies and Coat of Arms were added by George II.

◂● *Enter Outer Green Court. Proceed ahead to the moat and bridge passing the old barracks L.*

| Location 2 | **MOAT AND BRIDGE** |

The moat was filled and its bridge buried by Charles II. They were rediscovered in 1910. Henry VIII had built the bridge to replace an earlier structure.

Its parapets have been renewed. The Queen's (or King's) Beasts, flanking the bridge, are replacements carved in 1950.

◂● *Cross the bridge to the Great Gatehouse.*

| Location 3 | **GREAT GATEHOUSE** |

This was built for Wolsey and was originally two storeys higher and surmounted by cupolas and weather-vanes. The structure was shortened and remodelled in 1772 and refaced in the 19C.

The roundels of Roman emperors by *Maiano*, c.1521, were brought from Windsor. They may be those which originally decorated the Holbein Gate at Whitehall Palace.

On the oriel window are the arms of Henry VIII (renewed).

Flanking the Gatehouse range are two projecting wings which were extended later. The stone weasels on their battlements are original although much restored.

Oak doors to the Gatehouse are Tudor but its vault was renewed in 1882.

◂● *Pass through to Base Court.*

| Location 4 | **BASE COURT** |

On this side of the Gatehouse, the arms of Henry VIII, above the arch, have also been renewed.

Both turrets bear the arms of Elizabeth I.

All the buildings in this court are from Wolsey's period and formed an extension to Clock Court that lies further east. Henry VIII's Great Hall appears in the background ahead L.

◂● *Continue eastward to 'Anne Boleyn's' Gateway.*

HAMPTON COURT GREEN
HAMPTON COURT RD
BUSHEY PARK
HAMPTON COURT ROAD
0 100 Metres 300
0 500 Feet 1000
N
THE MAZE
TILTYARD TOWER
RIVER
THAMES
HAMPTON COURT BRIDGE
For locations 2–14 see plan below
Hampton Court Station
LANDING STAGE
PRIVY GARDEN
THE BROAD WALK
ROAD
BRIDGE
1
15
16
17
18
19
20
21
22
23
24
25
26
27
28
29
30
31
32
33
34

N
MOAT
MOAT
GREAT VINE
BASE COURT
MANTEGNA GALLERY
ANNE BOLEYNS GATEWAY
GREAT HALL
CLOCK COURT
STATE ROOMS
CHAPEL ROYAL
FOUNTAIN COURT
THE BROAD WALK
TO TUDOR TENNIS COURT
0 Metres 50
0 Feet 150
2
3
4
5
6
7
8
9
10
11
12
13
14
15
16
20
21
22
26
27
28
29

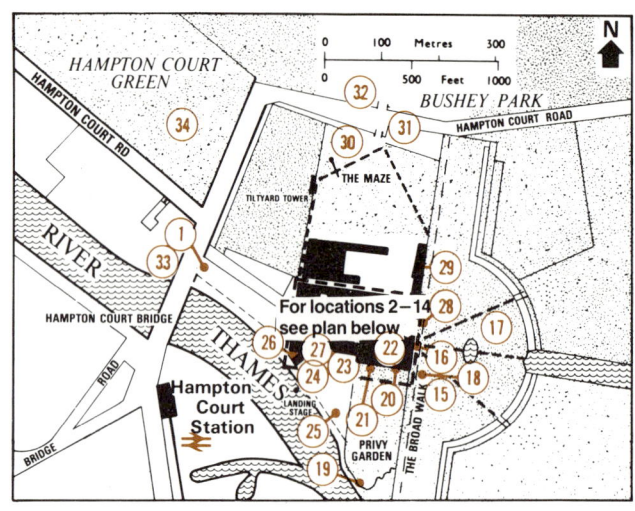

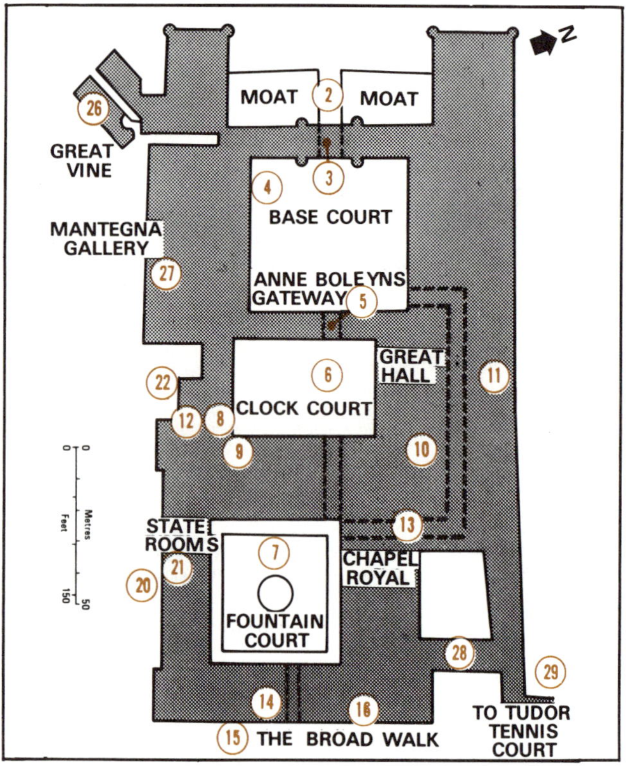

Hampton Court

Locations
1. Trophy Gates
2. Moat and bridge
3. Great Gatehouse
4. Base Court
5. 'Anne Boleyn's' Gateway
6. Clock Court
7. Fountain Court
8. The Building of Hampton Court Exhibition
9. State Rooms
10. Wine Cellar
11. Great Kitchens
12. Renaissance Picture Gallery and Wolsey Rooms
13. Chapel Royal Entranceway
14. King's Private Apartments
15. Broad Walk
16. East Façade of Wren's Building
17. Fountain Garden
18. East Grounds
19. Tijou Screens
20. South Façade of Wren's Building
21. Upper Orangery
22. South Façade of the Tudor Building
23. Knot Garden
24. Pond Garden
25. Banqueting House
26. Vinery
27. Lower Orangery (Mantegna Cartoons)
28. Old Close Tennis Court
29. 'Tudor' Tennis Court
30. Maze
31. Lion Gate
32. Bushy Park
33. The Mitre
34. Hampton Court Green

Location 5	**'ANNE BOLEYN'S' GATEWAY**

This was built by Wolsey but is named after Henry's second queen, probably because it was embellished during Anne's brief reign.

The 18C bell turret houses one bell dating from 1480.

The clock, made in 1799, was brought from St James's Palace in 1835 to replace the west face of the Astronomical Clock which was lost during restoration.

Above the arch are the arms of Henry VIII.

The two roundels of Roman emperors are part of a set of eight made for Hampton Court by *Giovanni da Maiano* in 1521. The others are seen later. They are an early example of Italian Renaissance work in England.

Beneath the arch, on two small bosses, the 'H' and 'A' monograms (Henry VIII and Anne Boleyn) in the ceiling, were restored with the vaulting in 1882.

☛ *Pass through the gateway to Clock Court.*

Location 6	**CLOCK COURT**

On the other side of Anne Boleyn's Gateway is the east face of the Astronomical Clock which was made, in England, by the Frenchman *Nicholas Oursian* in 1540. Its mechanism was renewed in 1879. The dial, 7ft 10in in diameter, indicates the hour, day, month, moon phase and time of high water at London Bridge. The last information was most important when the main approach to Hampton Court was by water. In the centre, the sun is depicted revolving around the earth as it was believed to in the 16C.

Above the arch are Wolsey's arms in 16C Italian terracotta work, incorporating his cardinal's hat. The arms were defaced by Henry VIII but have been restored.

Two further roundels by *Maiano* are seen.

6   Hampton Court

It is believed that Wolsey began his manor house on part of the site of this court and much of the west side, with Anne Boleyn's Gateway, dates from this period. He later extended this range southward.

Henry's Great Hall L occupies all the north side. It was built by *John Moulton* in 1534 and incorporates the site of Wolsey's original, more modest hall. The bay window may have been re-used from that building.

Behind *Wren*'s 17C colonnade, on the south side, are the Building of Hampton Court Exhibition and Renaissance Picture Galleries. Return later to visit them. These rooms occupy the second of the south ranges built by Wolsey when the courtyard was extended southward. Paving in front of the colonnade indicates the line of the earlier range.

The east façade ahead was remodelled for George II by *Kent* in 1732. It is an early example of Neo-Gothic work which was insisted on, allegedly by Prime Minister Walpole, to harmonize with the remainder of the court. The range was remodelled further in 1844.

The George II Gateway is embellished with more roundels. Originally, a high building stood here with private suites on three floors. These became the royal apartments until Henry built more extensive accommodation further east. Some of the Tudor fabric remains.

•● *Pass through the gateway towards Fountain Court. Wren's Queen's Stairway is seen L but may not be entered at this point.*

| Location 7 | **FOUNTAIN COURT** |

The contrast between Wren's Classical court, completed in 1694, and those seen previously comes as a surprise. It was planned as the core of William and Mary's new palace and is built on the site of the slightly smaller Cloister Green Court which Henry had added to Wolsey's building to accommodate his royal apartments.

The State Apartments and Queen's Private Apartments are on the first floor. Above and below them were the apartments of the staff, courtiers and guests.

The ground floor of the south range housed the King's Private Apartments.

Surrounds to the circular windows were carved by *Cibber*.

•● *Proceed ahead to the barrier and then return to Clock Court L. (Do not exit to the grounds at this point as re-entry from the east side is prohibited due to security checks.) Enter the Building of Hampton Court Exhibition from Clock Court's colonnade.*

| Location 8 | **BUILDING OF HAMPTON COURT EXHIBITION** |

Open April–September. Admission free.

The recently enlarged exhibition describes the evolution of Hampton Court.

•● *Exit L and proceed to the ticket office for entry*

Hampton Court 7

tickets to the State Rooms and Renaissance Picture Galleries. Return along the colonnade to the entrance to the State Rooms in the south-east corner.

Location 9	**STATE ROOMS**

Open daily. Admission charge. NB: retain the ticket for admission to the King's Private Apartments and the Banqueting House.

Following the fire in 1986, some rooms will be temporarily closed for renovation and the route followed may change from time to time. The rooms affected are indicated by an asterisk.

On Mary's death in 1694 the sorrowing William immediately halted all work and interior decoration did not commence until 1699. William died in 1702, with only the King's Apartments and Queen's Gallery completed. Most of the Queen's Apartments were eventually decorated for Queen Anne but some later work dates from the reigns of George I and George II.

Great craftsmen who worked on the apartments included carver *Gibbons*, ironsmith *Tijou*, painter *Verrio* (he died at Hampton Court in 1707), and later, designers *Vanbrugh* and *Kent*. Some of the furnishings and paintings remain in their original positions.

At present, the rooms are seen in almost precisely reverse chronological order. Visited first are the King's State Apartments, on the south side, in the order that courtiers would have proceeded. The King's private rooms are situated below on the ground floor and may be seen later. The Queen's State Apartments, on the east and north sides, are then entered in reverse order to the original approach. Her private rooms are on the same floor adjacent to these facing Fountain Court. Before all the Queen's rooms have been seen, a brief detour is made to part of the Tudor section via the Cartoon Gallery. Finally, the major surviving Tudor buildings are entered.

The name of each State Room is written in gold above its exit door.

As the most important rooms, together with their contents, are described on display panels and the paintings are titled, only a selection will be described in this book.

King's Staircase. Completed after William's death. The balustrade is by *Tijou* and the wall paintings are by *Verrio*.

King's Guardroom. Yeomen of the Guard originally stood on duty here. Over 3000 pieces of arms are displayed, all as originally arranged in the 17C.

King's First Presence Chamber. The chair is 17C but a replacement.

Only the carving above the door is by *Gibbons*.

•● *Proceed through the* **King's Second Presence Chamber**.

King's Audience Chamber.* This chair is 17C, but also a replacement; the decorated sections of the pier glasses (mirrors) are original.

King's Drawing Room.* The overmantel is by *Gibbons*.

King William III's State Bedchamber.* The ceiling was painted by *Verrio*.

The state bed, chairs and stools are original.

A rare 17C close stool (commode) retains its original upholstery.

Tapestries are from the 16C Abraham series; the remainder are seen later.

The cornice by *Gibbons* is judged some of his finest work.

King's Dressing Room.* William III generally slept here, rather than in the more public State Bedchamber.

The ceiling is by *Verrio*.

The furniture is not original to the room.

•● *Proceed through the* **King's Writing Closet.***

Queen Mary's Closet.* This room was never, of course, used by Queen Mary but at one time the walls were hung with her needlework.

Queen's Gallery. This was designed as an art gallery to display the Mantegna cartoons which now hang in the Lower Orangery, seen later. It was the last room to be completed before William's death.

The cornice and doorcases are by *Gibbons*.

Tapestries from the Alexander series are Flemish, made in the 18C to designs of *Lebrun* executed in 1662. They were probably fitted here for George I.

The fireplace, judged outstanding, was brought from the King's Bedchamber in 1701. It was carved by *John Nost*.

Queen's Bedchamber. This room was decorated and furnished for the Prince and Princess of Wales (later George II and Queen Caroline).

The ceiling, painted by *Thornhill* in 1715, had been whitewashed over but is now restored.

The bed retains part of its rare 18C upholstery.

The chairs and stools were made in 1716.

Queen's Drawing Room. This room was decorated for Queen Anne by *Verrio* in 1705.

Comprehensive views of the Baroque *patte d'oie* (goose-foot) layout of the east grounds are obtained from the windows.

Queen's Audience Chamber. This chamber was decorated for George II when Prince of Wales.

One of the 16C tapestries from the Abraham series is hung, the remainder are in the Great Hall, seen later.

The chandelier was made in 1707 to commemorate the union of England and Scotland.

Public Dining Room. This was decorated as a music room by *Vanbrugh* c.1718 for George II but it eventually became a dining room where the king would occasionally eat in public.

The cornice and arms of George I on the chimney-piece are by *Gibbons*.

Prince of Wales's Suite. This suite of three rooms was decorated for Queen Anne by *Vanbrugh* but first used in 1716 by George II when Prince of Wales.

In the last room of this suite, the **bedroom**, Charlotte's bed, *c.*1778, has been fitted with new covers which incorporate the original embroidery.

The **Queen's Private Apartments** consist of a series of small panelled rooms.

■● *Pass the* **Prince of Wales's Staircase**.

George II's Private Chamber. The flock wallpaper, *c.*1730, is original to the room.

Cartoon Gallery.* The gallery, by *Wren* 1699, lies behind the King's State Apartments. It was planned for the display of seven cartoons, painted by *Raphael* in 1516, part of a series of ten illustrating the lives of St Peter and St Paul. These were produced as designs for tapestries commissioned for the Vatican's Sistine Chapel. Charles I purchased the cartoons for Hampton Court but they are now displayed in the Victoria and Albert Museum. The 17C Mortlake tapestries that now hang in this gallery were copied from the cartoons.

All the carving, including the chimney-piece, is by *Gibbons*.

Communication Gallery. This gallery linked the King's and Queen's State Apartments.

The 17C portraits by *Lely* are of ladies from Charles II's Court. They originally hung at Windsor Castle and are still known as 'The Windsor Beauties'.

■● *At the end of the gallery a door L leads to some Tudor rooms.*

Wolsey's Closet. The panels were painted in the 16C over 15C work, presumably brought from elsewhere.

On the original 16C ceiling is painted Wolsey's motto 'Dominus Michi Adjutor' (The Lord is my helper).

The 16C linenfold panelling was fitted here in 1886.

Cumberland Suite. This series of rooms was briefly occupied by a son of George II, the Duke of Cumberland, 'Butcher Cumberland of Culloden'. Some of the wall fabric is Tudor but the interior was completely remodelled for George II by *Kent* in 1732.

Windows and one ceiling are in the Neo-Gothic style.

■● *Return to Wren's building and turn L.*

Queen's Staircase. The balustrade is by *Tijou* and most of the walls and ceiling were painted by *Kent*. The 'Apollo' wall painting of 1628 is by *Honthorst*.

■● *Turn immediately R.*

Queen's Guard Chamber. On the walls are hung the 18C paintings known as 'The Hampton Court Beauties' by *Kneller*.

Queen's Presence Chamber. Decorated for George I by *Vanbrugh*, most of the carving is by *Gibbons*.

The furniture comes from Windsor Castle and was made for Queen Anne in 1714.

● Return to the Queen's Staircase, turn R and enter the most important Tudor section of the palace.

Haunted Gallery. This gallery, redecorated in the 18C, linked the Chapel Royal with Wolsey's state apartments. It is reputedly haunted by Catherine Howard, Henry VIII's fifth wife, who was executed for adultery. Under arrest, it is alleged that she escaped from her room and ran along this corridor screaming for Henry, who was at prayer in the chapel nearby.

● The door R leads to the gallery of the Chapel Royal.

Holyday Closets. On either side of the Royal Pew are two pews used by the king and queen, known as the Holyday Closets.

The first entered has a Tudor ceiling, much restored.

Royal Pew. This pew was redecorated for Queen Anne by *Wren* in 1711 and the ceiling painted by *Thornhill*. From here the interior of the Chapel Royal, not open to visitors, may be viewed.

Chapel Royal. Although the chapel was built for Wolsey, little survives internally from his period. The timber-vaulted ceiling was added for Henry VIII in 1536 and redecorated in the 19C by *Pugin* who added the stars to the design.

Much of the chapel was remodelled by *Wren* early in the 18C.

The wooden reredos is by *Gibbons*; the painting above this is by *Thornhill*.

Wren's replacement windows were in their turn replaced in the 19C to match the originals.

● Return to the Haunted Gallery which continues R. Continue through the first room.

Great Watching Chamber. This was built for Henry VIII in 1536 as a guard room and is all that remains of his state apartments.

The panelled ceiling was restored in the 19C. Some of its bosses incorporate the arms of Henry and his third wife, Jane Seymour.

The early-16C Flemish tapestries were probably purchased by Wolsey.

The bay window has been renewed.

All the stained glass in this chamber is 19C.

The entrance with double doors to the hall was added in the 19C.

●▶ *Enter the hall and proceed directly to the first door R; this leads to the Horn Room.*

Horn Room. From here, food was served to the high table.

Original oak steps still lead directly to the kitchen and cellars below.

The ceiling was initially painted.

●▶ *Return to the hall.*

Great Hall. The Great Hall, 1554, replaced Wolsey's original hall and was Henry VIII's most important addition to Hampton Court. Leading members of the household feasted at a high table set on the raised dais but the king generally dined within his private apartments. Others ate at common tables set along the side walls.

Incorporated in the hammerbeam roof by *Nedeham* are the monograms and badges of Anne Boleyn and Jane Seymour.

The design of its hanging pendants reflects a Renaissance influence.

Originally, an open hearth stood in the centre of the hall and smoke escaped from its fire through a vent in the roof, since filled in.

The Abraham tapestries are Flemish, made in 1540. They are threaded with gold and silver.

At the far end of the hall, above an oak screen, the minstrels' gallery, although basically Tudor, has been much restored.

The screen is original and was built to obscure the servants' passage.

●▶ *Exit to the foot of the stairs R and pass through Anne Boleyn's Gateway. Take the first path R keeping to the east side of Base Court. Continue through the arch in the north-east corner ahead. Proceed R along North Cloister (a dark passage). Enter the fourth door R.*

Location 10	**WINE CELLAR**

The vaulting is of plastered brickwork. In Tudor times all the wine drunk at Hampton Court was imported although the beer was brewed on the premises. Modern casks illustrate the stillages, a typical Tudor arrangement.

●▶ *Exit L. First R is the entrance to Service Place and the kitchens.*

Location 11	**GREAT KITCHENS**

These are the most extensive examples of Tudor kitchens to survive and were in use until the 18C. Food cooked here on open fires was passed through hatches into Serving Place and thence up the stairs to the Horn Room. It was then taken to the high table in the Great Hall and the royal apartments.

The first kitchen entered was built for Wolsey but most of the utensils exhibited are 18C.

12 Hampton Court

The next two kitchens were added by Henry in 1529 to serve the common tables in the Great Hall. Originally they formed one room but were subdivided in the 17C. Their ceilings were lowered c.1840.

The third room was converted into an apartment in the 19C and some fittings from this period have been retained, e.g. the range with its boiler.

● Exit from the kitchens and proceed ahead keeping to the west side of Base Court. Return L through the Anne Boleyn Gateway to Clock Court. The entrance to the Renaissance Picture Gallery and Wolsey Rooms is beneath the colonnade. From The King's Staircase, proceed along the ground floor passage, known as Stone Hall, to the Beauty Staircase.

● Alternatively, proceed ahead from Clock Court to Fountain Court and the Chapel Royal entranceway (Location 13).

Location 12

RENAISSANCE PICTURE GALLERY AND WOLSEY ROOMS

Open daily. Admission charge.

Beauty Staircase. The staircase was named from the paintings of 'The Windsor Beauties' by *Lely* which formerly hung in the king's adjacent private dining room but are now in the Communication Gallery previously described.

● Ascend the stairs and enter the Tudor building.

The first two rooms were remodelled in the 18C and again in the 20C.

Tapestries are 17C Italian.

Wolsey Rooms. These rooms were most probably occupied by guests or senior household members, but possibly by Wolsey himself. The two rooms R were originally one but sub-divided in the 17C.

The 16C linenfold panelling is original.

In the second room are remnants of a stone Tudor doorway in the corner.

● Return to the central room.

This has a 16C ribbed ceiling, recently restored. Its design was influenced by the Renaissance.

The fourth room also has a restored 16C ceiling which incorporates Wolsey's badge.

The windows in this room are 18C.

● Cross the lobby.

Renaissance Picture Gallery. Renaissance paintings on wood from the royal collection are displayed. These rooms were probably once occupied by an important member of the Court. They were mainly refitted in the 17C but some fragments of Tudor doorways and panelling remain.

Beyond are two rooms which have been decorated as a Victorian 'grace and favour' residence.

● Return along the corridor and descend the

Elizabethan spiral staircase. Exit R and proceed from Clock Court to Fountain Court. Turn immediately L and proceed beneath the arch. Enter the door R to the Chapel Royal.

Location 13	**CHAPEL ROYAL ENTRANCEWAY**

The chapel is only open for services.

Above the door are the arms of Henry VIII and Catherine Parr, his sixth wife, who outlived him.

The interior has already been described as seen from the Royal Pew.

•• *Return to Fountain Court. On the east side is the vestibule with the entrance R to the King's Private Apartments. Do not exit yet from this vestibule into the grounds.*

Location 14	**KING'S PRIVATE APARTMENTS**

Open April–September. Admission by ticket for the State Apartments.

This suite is connected with the King's State Apartments above, by a private staircase. The long Cartoon Gallery on the first floor left no space for the king's private rooms to run, like the queen's, adjacent to the State Apartments.

Little is known about their use or furnishing and William III probably only ever occupied a few of them. They were remodelled in the 19C to form grace and favour residences.

Some of the furniture in the rooms is contemporary with William III's reign. Paintings from the Royal Collection, together with ancient prints of Hampton Court, are displayed.

•• *Exit from the Apartments and return to the vestibule.*

The three iron screens R are by *Tijou*.

•• *Exit to the east grounds.*

Location 15	**BROAD WALK**

This gravel path, running north to south (L to R), was laid out by *Wise*, c.1700, to separate the Fountain Garden and Privy Garden.

Location 16	**EAST FAÇADE OF WREN'S BUILDING**

The low height of the ground floor was designed so that the asthmatic William would not have to climb too many stairs.

Portland stone carvings by *Cibber* include the central 'Hercules' pediment.

Location 17	**FOUNTAIN GARDEN**

This parterre, with yew trees, immediately fronts the east façade. It is a restoration of the formal garden originally laid out as a *patte d'oie* (goose-foot) pattern for William III by *Loudon* and *Wise*. Initially, there were thirteen fountains but only a pool remains.

The statues are 19C.

•• *Continue eastward along any path to the semi-circular canal.*

14   Hampton Court

Location 18	**EAST GROUNDS**

These grounds were laid out for Charles II by *Mollet* in the Classical Baroque style, pre-dating all of Wren's work at Hampton Court.

The Long Water, when completed, almost reached the palace but it was shortened later to form William's Fountain Garden.

The iron gates to the three avenues are by *Tijou*.

The semi-circular canal around the lime trees was added for Queen Anne.

☛ *Proceed to the south-east corner of Wren's building. The gate R leads to the south grounds. Immediately L is the Privy Garden.*

This garden was also laid out as a parterre in 1701 but has been much altered.

☛ *Follow the central alley, known as Queen Mary's Bower, through the garden towards the river and proceed to the end.*

Location 19	**TIJOU SCREENS**

These twelve wrought iron panels, judged some of Tijou's finest work, were brought here from the Fountain Garden in 1701.

☛ *Return to the south façade.*

Location 20	**SOUTH FAÇADE OF WREN'S BUILDING**

Carved to form the stone centrepiece above the window are the names, in Latin, of William and Mary.

Below this, the cherubs and royal coats of arms are by *Cibber*.

Originally the blind circular windows were decorated with paintings by *Laguerre*.

☛ *Pass through the central gates and proceed to the entrance to the Upper Orangery.*

Location 21	**UPPER ORANGERY**
Open April-September.	When built, orange trees were kept here in the winter and the building has recently been restored as an orangery.

☛ *Exit R to the end of the terrace and pass through the gate.*

Location 22	**SOUTH FAÇADE OF THE TUDOR BUILDING**

Immediately R, the bay window, adjoining Wren's buildings, displays 'ER 1568' on its stone work. This denotes rebuilding in the reign of Elizabeth I.

Hampton Court 15

	The octagonal turret, L, is Tudor and the Wolsey Rooms are situated on the first floor behind and to the right of it.
	The decorative lead cupola has been restored.
Location 23	**KNOT GARDEN**
	This small area in front of the Elizabethan bay was planted in 1924 in the manner of a 16C garden.
Location 24	**POND GARDEN**
	On the L is the Old Pond Garden.
	•● *Follow the path to the Banqueting House at the river end.*
Location 25	**BANQUETING HOUSE**
Open April–September. Admission charge or included with State Apartments ticket.	A Tudor garden tower was converted, or probably completely rebuilt, for William by *Wren* in 1700 to accommodate summer banquets.
	•● *Enter the building.*
	Paintings are by *Verrio* and the door, mirror surround and window cases were carved by *Gibbons*.
	•● *Return northward towards the south façade of the Tudor building. Turn L.*
	Immediately L is the New Pond Garden. This was planted in 1925 following the 17C style.
	•● *Return again towards the south façade of the Tudor building. Turn L to the Vinery.*
Location 26	**VINERY**
	The Great Vine was planted in 1768. Grapes are still produced in late summer and may be purchased. A record crop in 1985 yielded 840lb. The girth of the trunk is 78in.
	•● *Exit L and proceed to the Lower Orangery.*
Location 27	**LOWER ORANGERY**
Open April–September. Admission charge.	Nine late-15C cartoons by *Mantegna* illustrate 'The Triumph of Caesar'. These were purchased by Charles I and are the world's oldest known paintings on canvas. All except one have been restored. They were originally displayed in the Queen's Gallery.
	•● *Exit L and return to the east façade of Wren's building. Continue to the end. Immediately L are the remains of the palace's Tudor east façade.*
Location 28	**OLD CLOSE TENNIS COURT**
Not open.	This building is buttressed and lies behind the garden wall. Added by Henry VIII, *c.*1530, it was remodelled in the late 17C, and converted to lodgings.
	•● *Continue ahead. Enter the first gate L.*

16 Hampton Court

Location 29	**'TUDOR' TENNIS COURT**
Open daily. Admission free.	This tennis court is not Tudor but was built c.1625, and later altered for Charles II.
	The windows are 18C.
	'Real' tennis, the predecessor of lawn tennis, is still played and matches may be viewed.
	Exit L. Proceed to the first gate L. Take the first path R and proceed ahead. Take the second path L towards the Maze.

Location 30	**MAZE**
Open March–October. Admission charge.	This was laid out in its present triangular shape in 1714, replacing an earlier circular version planned for William III as part of a formal garden known as The Wilderness.
	Exit L. First L Lion Gate.

Location 31	**LION GATE**
	The gate was built for Queen Anne as the north entrance to the palace grounds. Its design incorporates her cypher.
	Exit from the grounds and cross the road ahead.

Location 32	**BUSHY PARK**
	Although not part of Hampton Court grounds, the park with its chestnut avenue seen through the gates was planned by *Wren* as a grand approach to his projected, but never to be built, Classical north façade of the palace.
	The Diana Fountain by *Fanelli*, seen in the distance, was brought here from the Privy Garden in 1713.
	Deer roam the park which may be driven through.
	Return through the Lion Gate to the Hampton Court grounds. The second path R passes the Maze. Continue ahead towards the **tiltyard tower**.
	This is the only remaining example of the four towers which stood at the corners of Henry's tiltyard, where knights jousted.
	Follow the path L past the tower and continue ahead towards the palace. The path R leads to the Trophy Gates. Exit and cross the road.
	Alternatively, turn L and cross the bridge to Hampton Court Station (BR).

Location 33	**THE MITRE**
	The 17C Mitre Hotel faces the palace. Its façade was remodelled early in the 19C and little of interest survives internally.
	Proceed northward to Hampton Court Green first L. Follow its south side.

| Location 34 | **HAMPTON COURT GREEN** |

Palace Gate House is mid 18C.

The Green is early 18C with a later bay.

The Old Court House *Wren c.1706 (?)*. Occupied by Wren from 1706 until his death in 1723. It was his official residence as Surveyor General. The upper floor and bay window are later additions.

Faraday House. Michael Faraday, discoverer of electricity, retired here from 1858 until his death in 1867.

•● *Take the first drive L signposted 'TMYC'. Proceed to the end L.*

King's Stone Cottage. The weather-boarded 18C house is topped with a weathervane.

Above the drainpipe is George III's monogram.

•● *Return along the drive L.*

Tudor Royal Mews. This long, arcaded range encompasses a cobbled courtyard. Here the royal horses were stabled. It was built in 1538 and extended in 1570; much remodelling followed.

•● *Cross Hampton Court Bridge to Hampton Court Station (BR).*

•● *Alternatively, follow the towpath to the landing stage for boats to Richmond and London.*

Richmond

Richmond possesses some of the finest Queen Anne and early Georgian domestic properties in England. Remnants of the great Tudor royal palace survive, facing its green. While an important part of the riverside will be under redevelopment for some years, its path still provides what is probably the most attractive stretch along the Thames in the vicinity of London. From the top of Richmond Hill can be gained the famous view of the sylvan Thames curving towards old Twickenham. Immediately south of the hill are the 2000 acres of Richmond Park, by far the largest of all the London boroughs' royal parks.

Timing Any day is suitable as there are no great buildings to be entered. Fine weather would be a great advantage.

Suggested connections To explore Richmond thoroughly will occupy most of a day but it could be preceded by a brief visit to Kew Gardens or continued with Ham and Petersham.

20 Richmond

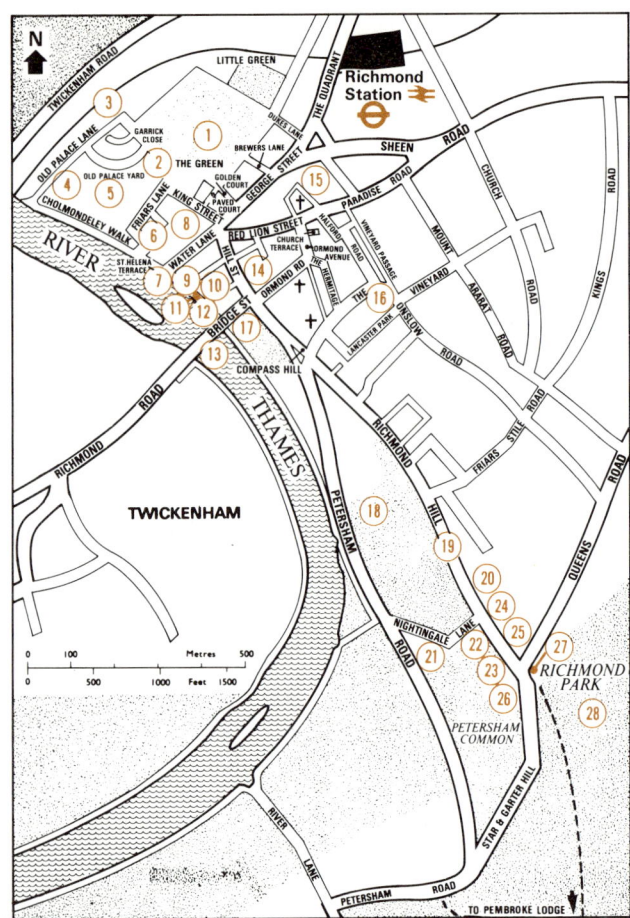

Locations
1. Richmond Green
2. Richmond Palace
3. Old Palace Lane
4. Asgill House
5. Trumpeter's House
6. St Helena Terrace
7. White Cross Inn
8. Water Lane
9. Riverside, Water Lane to Richmond Bridge
10. Old Town Hall
11. Heron House
12. Tower House
13. Richmond Bridge
14. Ormond Road
15. St Mary Magdalen
16. The Vineyard
17. Riverside, Richmond Bridge to the Terrace Gardens
18. Terrace Gardens
19. Richmond Hill
20. No 3 The Terrace
21. The Petersham Hotel
22. The Wick
23. Wick House
24. Richmond Hill Hotel
25. Richmond Gate Hotel
26. Royal Star and Garter Home
27. Ancaster House
28. Richmond Park

Richmond 21

Start *Richmond Station (BR), District Line or from Waterloo Station (BR). Exit from the station and cross The Quadrant immediately L. Take the footpath first R through the Oriel House archway. First L cross the railway bridge to Little Green.*

Location 1	**RICHMOND GREEN**

Richmond Green is regarded by many as the finest in the country, as it is bounded on two sides by outstanding examples of five centuries of building styles. Unfortunately, houses on the east side have almost all been converted to offices.

The green once faced Richmond Palace and was a knights' jousting ground. Following the Civil War, the palace fell into disrepair and Richmond was briefly abandoned by the Court. Royalty returned to the area in the late 17C when William III purchased what was later to become Ormond Lodge in the old Deer Park, and Richmond Green become, once again, a fashionable address. As at Kew Green, cricket is played here in the summer. The south and east sides are of prime architectural interest.

Immediately R is Little Green, once waste land, granted by Charles II for bowling.

Richmond Theatre *Matcham*, 1899, faces Little Green. It retains a late Victorian interior.

•● *Continue southward along the east side of the green to the Duke's Lane corner. On the corner is No 1, The Green.*

No 1 was built early in the 17C but has been much altered. By tradition, it was the residence of Simon Bardolph, friend of William Shakespeare, who reputedly stayed with him during his visits to Richmond Palace. Bardolph is buried in the parish church.

No 3, Gothic House, was also built in the early 17C. Its façade has been renewed in Neo-Gothic style. Then follows **No 4**, early 18C and **No 5** early 19C.

No 6 was completed recently, in Post-Modernist style, for architects *Darbourne & Darke*, of course by themselves.

No 7 is early 18C with Victorian additions.

No 8 and **9** are mid 18C.

Nos 10–12 are early 18C. All have fine eaves and **No 11, Queen's House**, and **No 12** also possess exceptional porches.

•● *L Brewers Lane.*

Brewers Lane has Richmond's largest concentration of antique shops.

•● *Return to The Green L.*

Nos 15, 16, 17, 22 and **23** are early 18C.

•● *Pass the entrance to Golden Court (of little interest) and continue ahead to Paved Court.*

Paved Court. Many late-17C properties survive in what is Richmond Green's most attractive alleyway. Demolition was proposed in the 1960s but a letter sent to the *Richmond and*

Twickenham Times by the author of this book instigated a campaign by conservationists which proved successful.

No 1, at the far end R, retains an early-19C bow window.

•● *Return to Richmond Green L and proceed westward.*

Nos 31 and **32** are early 18C.

•● *The east side again turns southward and is called Old Palace Terrace.*

Old Palace Terrace 1692 is an early example of a speculative development.

•● *Cross the road immediately ahead to the south side of Richmond Green.*

Oak House *c*.1769. This is believed to have been built by *Robert Taylor*, who had previously designed Asgill House on the riverside, Richmond's most distinguished villa (Location 4).

•● *Turn R and proceed westward.*

Old Palace Place. This was built in the Tudor period but remodelled *c*.1700. A 16C wall painting survives internally.

Old Friars 1687. The cellars of this house were built *c*.1500 and survive from an earlier building which stood on the site. A rear extension R was built *c*.1740, possibly as a music or assembly room.

•● *Proceed to Friars Lane, first L.*

Friars Lane. This divided the Convent of the Observant Friars, a monastery established by Henry VII *c*.1500, from Richmond Palace. No trace of its buildings remains.

No 44, Tudor House and **Tudor Place.** These two houses were originally built in the 18C as one dwelling. Side porches are later additions.

Maids of Honour Row 1724. This terrace of four houses was built by the future George II to accommodate the maids of honour serving his wife, Caroline of Anspach, Princess of Wales, who then lived at Ormond Lodge in Old Deer Park.

•● *Continue past The Old Palace and Palace Gatehouse, both remnants of Richmond Palace which is described later (Location 2).*

The Old Court House. The bow window was added early in the 19C to this early-18C house.

Wentworth House. Also built in the 18C, it was originally identical to the Old Court House but was remodelled by *Laxton c*.1858.

•● *Pass Garrick Close (the site of an earlier Richmond theatre) and cross to the corner house on the west side of the green.*

The Virginals 1813. This was built as Cedar Grove on the site of the palace bakehouse.

Pembroke Villas. On the west side of the green,

Richmond 23

these were built *c*.1850 on the site of Pembroke House and its grounds.

• Return towards the old gateway to Richmond Palace. Immediately L, facing the Green, are two adjoining houses, The Old Palace and Palace Gatehouse.

Location 2	**RICHMOND PALACE**
Richmond Green	All that survives of the great Tudor palace are its gateway and some brickwork forming the walls of adjacent buildings, now private houses.

Richmond Palace was built on the site of three earlier royal residences, the first being the 12C Shene manor house which Henry I acquired in 1125. Edward III died there in 1377; Anne of Bohemia, Richard II's first consort, also died at the palace, of the plague, in 1394, and the King, deranged by grief, immediately demolished most of the building. A new Shene Palace was begun by Henry V but not completed until 1462. This burnt down in 1497.

Henry VII, in a rare burst of extravagance, then commissioned, on the 10-acre site, the largest, and at the time most magnificent, of all the Tudor royal palaces. Henry had previously been Duke of Richmond (Yorkshire) and he renamed the palace Richmond, dying there in 1509. After assigning Hampton Court to Henry VIII in 1529, Wolsey was given permission to reside at the palace. Richmond was particularly favoured by Elizabeth I, who also died here in 1603. Prince Henry, the eldest son of James I, lived at Richmond until his premature and unexplained death, which prevented him from inheriting the throne. His brother, Charles I, stayed at Richmond during the plague year of 1625, but following the Civil War, Oliver Cromwell stripped the palace of all its finery and demolished the most important buildings. Charles II preferred Windsor, and although his mother, Henrietta Maria, lodged at Richmond she did not like it and soon moved to Greenwich. James II's children lived at the palace during their infancy and its restoration by Wren was planned. With the King's exile, however, the scheme was abandoned and royalty finally left Richmond Palace.

The Old Palace and Palace Gatehouse. The joint north façades of these two houses once formed part of the external wall of the palace. Much remodelling has taken place, including the 18C addition to Palace Gatehouse of its large bay.

• Proceed to the gateway.

Gateway. Above the large arch are the arms, renewed, of Henry VII. It has been implausibly alleged that Elizabeth I died in the small room above the arch.

• Proceed through the gateway to Old Palace Yard. Immediately L is the west façade of Palace Gatehouse.

The stair turret is believed to be original.

24 Richmond

A link between Palace Gatehouse and The Wardrobe was built in the 17C.

The Wardrobe. In this building were originally stored the palace's furnishings and hangings. Although now converted to provide three houses, much of the brickwork is original.

Clearly visible are Tudor arches, bricked in, probably in the 17C.

The west (garden) façade of this range was completely remodelled in Classical style, c.1708, allegedly by *Wren*. This can only be seen on the rare occasions when the gardens are open to visitors in support of charities.

Old Palace Yard was the outer courtyard of the palace. Two further courtyards lay ahead between this point and the river. Trumpeter's House in the south-east corner occupies the site of the Middle Gateway, through which visitors passed to the Middle Court.

Trumpeter's House (north façade) 1701. Some of the fabric is Tudor and may have belonged to the Middle Gateway. There is no evidence that Wren worked on the house as has been alleged. The residence was originally known as Trumpeting House, from two stone trumpeters that decorated the façade. Austrian Chancellor Metternich lived here in 1848, and the house later became the residence of radio pioneer Marconi. The building was restored and converted to flats in 1952. Its south façade is seen later.

•● *Continue westward. Second L Old Palace Lane.*

Location 3	**OLD PALACE LANE**

This terrace of small cottages was built c.1810.

The **White Swan** inn, towards the river end, possesses a beamed interior and a rear patio for summer drinking.

•● *Exit R to the river. L Cholmondeley Walk. Asgill House overlooks the river immediately L.*

Location 4	**ASGILL HOUSE** R. Taylor 1758
Cholmondeley Walk	This Palladian villa was built in stone for Sir Charles Asgill, Lord Mayor of London and a friend of the architect. It occupies the site of the old palace brewhouse that stood outside the walls. The house, the most outstanding example of *Sir Robert Taylor*'s work near London, was restored in 1969.
Open by appointment but only to ratepayers of Richmond-upon-Thames.	

•● *Continue ahead.*

In the south-east corner of the grounds is an 18C castellated summerhouse. Seen in the middle distance L is the south façade of Trumpeter's House.

Location 5	**TRUMPETER'S HOUSE SOUTH FAÇADE** 1701

Trumpeter's House's north façade has already been seen. This, the river front, is more impressive.

Richmond 25

The portico was added c.1722.

Both end pavilions were built in the mid 18C.

The lawn occupies the site of the private royal apartments of Richmond Palace that overlooked the river.

● Continue ahead.

Passed L are two mid-18C houses (**Nos 2** and **1** Cholmondeley Walk) with flood defences.

Location 6	**ST HELENA TERRACE c.1835**

The terrace, approached by steps, was built with private boat houses below. Its name commemorates the island where Napoleon was exiled.

Location 7	**WHITE CROSS INN c.1840**
Cholmondeley Walk	The top storey was added in 1865.

From the river bar, a window provides a good view of Richmond Bridge. Below this window, surprisingly, is the fireplace. Its flue turns to one side before ascending.

● Exit L. Proceed to Water Lane (first L).

Location 8	**WATER LANE**

Laid out in the mid-17C, this was known as Town Lane until 1712.

On the east side are 18C and 19C warehouses, converted to flats in 1985.

Most paving stones are of granite and were laid to support the loads deposited by watermen.

● Continue ahead.

Location 9	**RIVERSIDE, WATER LANE TO RICHMOND BRIDGE**

The large area bounded by Water Lane, the river, Bridge Street and Hill Street, has been neglected for many years due to planning disputes. It is being developed to provide offices, flats and shops. A few of the original façades are to be retained or reproduced.

● Proceed ahead.

Location 10	**OLD TOWN HALL** *Ancell 1893*

This lies to the north, and faces Hill Street. Second World War bombing destroyed its 'Renaissance' gables which were not renewed. The façade is to be preserved.

● Continue ahead. Heron House L is of five brick bays.

Location 11	**HERON HOUSE** *1693*

Built on the site of the royal mews, Heron House became, c.1806, the residence of Lady Hamilton and her daughter (by Nelson), Horatia. Some carved timbers discovered in the roof may have come from the Tudor Palace. The building was converted in 1858 to form part of the Royal (later

Palm Court) Hotel. Its last occupants were homeless mothers and their children who 'squatted' there in the late 1970s.

The external shell of this building and the adjacent 18C façade of the old Palm Court Hotel are to be retained.

● Continue ahead to the Tower House which overlooks Richmond Bridge.

Location 12	**TOWER HOUSE** *Laxton 1858*

With its distinguished Italianate tower, the house was restored in 1968 after conservationists had battled to save it from demolition.

Location 13	**RICHMOND BRIDGE** *Paine* and *Course 1777*

London's oldest remaining bridge is also judged its finest. The bridge, of Portland stone, replaced a horse ferry and was paid for by a toll. It was sensitively widened in 1937, and the addition, in paler stone, can be seen from beneath.

● Ascend the steps first L on the north side of the bridge. L Bridge St. First R Hill St. First L Ormond Rd.

● Alternatively, to shorten the itinerary, continue ahead beneath the bridge (Location 17).

Location 14	**ORMOND ROAD**

Immediately R is the early-18C Ormond Terrace. The front of **No 7** was remodelled in the late 18C.

Ormond House is also early 18C, but the doorway was replaced early in the 19C.

● Continue ahead to Ormond Avenue (first L).

The Rosary and **The Hollies** were both built by *Rawlins c.1700* as back-to-back houses.

● Cross the road and continue ahead.

The **Vicarage** was built in the early 19C, its porch is later.

● First L Church Terrace.

Although built in 1797, the **Bethlehem Chapel** was remodelled early in the 19C.

● Cross the road and continue northward.

Hermitage House was built *c.*1730 as was **Church Terrace** which follows immediately. The terrace is much altered.

● Cross Paradise Rd and follow the path to St Mary Magdalen's.

Location 15	**ST MARY MAGDALEN**
Paradise Road	St Mary Magdalen is renowned for its outstanding monuments.

This, the parish church of Richmond, is first recorded in 1211. It probably stood on the present site but no trace of that building remains. St Mary's was rebuilt in 1487 and its tower survives.

Tower. When completed c.1507, the tower is believed to have had only two stages, the third was probably added in 1624. It was entirely refaced with flint and stone in 1904.

The clock was added in 1812 but its dial is older (date unknown).

•● *Proceed to the west entrance.*

Both brick buildings, on either side of the entrance, providing porches, were added in 1864; stairs once led from them to the north and south galleries.

The entrance doorway is original.

•● *Turn L and proceed clockwise around the church.*

Nave north façade. A north aisle was added to the nave in 1699 but this disappeared when the nave was entirely rebuilt in 1750.

The present central window was formed in 1864. It replaced a north porch, which had been the main entrance. The brick cornice was added at the same time.

Against the wall is the obelisk commemorating Sir Mathew Decker by *Scheemakers*, 1759.

•● *Continue clockwise passing the* **vestry, chancel** *and* **south chapels.**

This eastern section was built by *Bodley* in 1904 when the small Tudor chancel was demolished.

•● *Continue to the south façade of the nave.*

Nave south façade. An aisle was added to this side of the nave in 1617. Like the later aisle, on the north side, it also disappeared when the nave was rebuilt in 1750. Unlike the north façade, there was no porch, instead there was a pediment above the central windows.

•● *Enter from the west door in the tower.*

Nave. The arch leading from the entrance porch to the nave is Tudor. No other part of the interior of the church pre-dates the rebuilding of 1750.

The roof was constructed by *A. W. Blomfield* in 1866.

Above the entrance are the royal arms.

•● *Turn L.*

On the west wall above the door is the monument to *John Bentley,* d. 1660, and his family, by *Burman* (?). It has been damaged and rearranged.

Below R is the monument to Shakespearian actor Edmund Kean by *Loft*, 1759. This originally stood outside the church which is the reason for its dilapidated condition.

Towards the east end of the north aisle, between the last two windows, is the monument to Robert Delafosse, d.1819, by *Flaxman*.

In the corner, before the organ, is the brass commemorating Robert Cotton, d.1591 (?). He

28 Richmond

was employed in the royal household of Mary I and Elizabeth I. It is the oldest monument in the church.

Above is the monument to Simon Bardolph, d.1654. He is believed to have been a friend of Shakespeare's and it is said that No 1 Richmond Green was his residence. Shakespeare used the name Bardolph for characters in *Henry V* and *The Merry Wives of Windsor*.

The organ by *Knight,* 1769, has been much rebuilt. It was transferred to its present position in the vestry from the west gallery in 1907. There were three galleries in the 18C; all have been removed.

The pulpit, L of the sanctuary, is believed to be late 17C.

•● *Proceed to the south aisle.*

The font has an 18C bowl, but its stem is modern.

Between the second and third windows from the east is the monument to the Hon Barbara Lowther, d.1805, by *Flaxman*.

•● *Continue to the south-west corner.*

A floor plaque marks the burial place, in the vault below, of Edmund Kean.

The monument to Major George Bean by *Bacon the Younger* commemorates an officer who was killed at the Battle of Waterloo in 1815.

Just before the exit L is the monument to Viscount Brounckner, d.1687, whom Pepys described as 'a pestilent rogue, an atheist that would have sold his king and country for 6d (3p) almost.'

•● *Exit from the church L and return to Paradise Rd L. Second R Halford Rd. Ahead, where the road bends, is Halford House.*

No 27, **Halford House**, was built in 1700. Its short eastward extension was added in 1745. The remainder of the street, although mid-Victorian, is basically Classical in style.

•● *L The Vineyard. At the Vineyard Passage corner (first L) is Vineyard House.*

Location 16	**THE VINEYARD**

This is one of the most picturesquely varied streets in the London area. It includes houses from the late 17C to the early 19C – some very grand – together with 19C almshouses and a Catholic church. Surprisingly, some light industry still survives. A vineyard probably stood here although none is recorded.

Vineyard House, early 18C, has a projecting wing to its garden. The doorway is late 18C.

•● *Return westward along The Vineyard and cross to the south side.*

Nos 29–23 are early-19C semi-detached houses.

On the opposite side, **Queen Elizabeth's Almshouses** were built in 1958. They replaced earlier almshouses of 1767, a plaque from which is inserted in the wall. Originally, the almshouses were founded in 1600 and stood further north in what is now Paradise Road.

Immediately opposite, on the north side, **No 11** is an early 19C villa.

Next to Queen Elizabeth's Almshouses are Bishop Duppa's Almshouses.

Bishop Duppa's Almshouses. A legacy from Bishop Brian Duppa founded these, originally on Richmond Hill, in 1661 as a thanks-offering for his deliverance from Oliver Cromwell. They were rebuilt here by *Little* in 1851. Some of the stonework and the gateway may have come from the earlier building.

Above the gate is an inscription, presumably composed by Duppa, 'I will pay the vows which I made to God in my troubles.'

Opposite, facing the street called The Hermitage, is an attractive villa **No 9**, **Newark House**, *c*.1750 with modern extensions.

Michel's Place, an early-19C terrace, follows.

Michel's Almshouses were founded on the same site in 1695, and rebuilt in 1811. The south range R was added in 1858.

No 2, Clarence House by *Rawlins*, *c*.1696, faces Michel's Almshouses. This is the grandest house in The Vineyard and is set back behind a courtyard surrounded by a high wall. It was, until recently, the home of actor Brian Blessed.

➠ First L Lancaster Park.

Vine Row 2–3 Lancaster Park. These two cottages, *c*.1700, are some of Richmond's oldest and most picturesque.

➠ Return to The Vineyard L. Cross the road to St Elizabeth's.

St Elizabeth of Portugal. This Roman Catholic Church was built in 1824, its tower, chancel and presbytery were rebuilt by *F. A. Walters* in 1903.

➠ Continue ahead. First L Richmond Hill. First R Compass Hill. The footpath R leads to Petersham Rd R. First L follow the path to the riverside walk L.

Location 17 | **RIVERSIDE, RICHMOND BRIDGE TO THE TERRACE GARDENS**

Many 18C mansions, with their riverside gardens, front the Petersham Road but their river façades have always been more important. Most are now converted to hotels.

Seen in the following order from the bridge is a terrace of late Victorian houses.

Nos 35 and **37** are early 19C.

No 39, **Bellevue**, with a pediment is late 18C.

No 42 is mid Victorian.

Nos 43–47, the **Hobart Hall Hotel**, was built in 1690 but has many 18C additions including castellation. William IV resided here, briefly, in 1789 while Duke of Clarence.

No 49 is a Victorian villa.

The adjoining public garden was once the site of another large house.

No 55, c.1720, has a Regency bay.

No 57–61, **The Paragon**, are also c.1720.

No 63, the **Bingham House Hotel**, is c.1760.

•● *Continue to the Raj Tavern (for many years the Three Pigeons). Take the path L, cross Petersham Rd and continue ahead through the Terrace Gardens. Follow any path up the hill to Richmond Hill.*

| Location 18 | **TERRACE GARDENS** |

These gardens were created in the mid 19C by *Walter Montagu-Douglas-Scott*. They then formed the grounds of his residence, Buccleuch House, which, together with the adjoining Lansdowne House, was demolished and the grounds acquired by the local authority for public gardens in 1886.

•● *At Richmond Hill turn R and cross the road.*

| Location 19 | **RICHMOND HILL** |

Many fine 18C residences on the brow of Richmond Hill enjoy one of England's most famous views.

Passed immediately is a mid-19C terrace, formerly the Stuart Hotel, but converted to flats in 1984.

No 114, **Norfolk House**, is mid 18C but its front was remodelled in the 19C.

No 116, **Downe House**, c.1771, was leased by the playright Sheridan early in the 19C.

No 118, **Ashburton**, is partly 18C but was remodelled in the 19C.

•● *Cross to the terrace opposite for the famous view.*

Many British artists, including J. M. W. Turner, have painted the view from Richmond Hill. On a clear day, Windsor Castle can be seen. It is claimed that Richmond, Virginia, USA, was so named because it possessed a similar view.

•● *Return to Richmond Hill R.*

Nos 120–122 are mid Victorian.

Nos 124–6 are early 19C.

No 128 is mid 19C.

The Roebuck inn was built in 1749 but its ground floor front has been altered.

Nos 1A, 1 and **2 The Terrace** are mid Victorian.

Richmond

Location 20	**NO 3 THE TERRACE** *Taylor (?) 1769*
Richmond Hill	Built in 1769 for a playing-card manufacturer, Christopher Blanchard. Mrs Fitzherbert lived here in the late 18C. She was secretly married by the vicar of Twickenham to the Prince of Wales, later George IV, in 1785 and it is alleged that they spent their honeymoon in this house.

Due to its style, the house is believed to be the work of *Sir Robert Taylor* the designer of Asgill House (Location 4). Its stone façade is one of Richmond's finest.

•● *Continue southward.*

No 4 The Terrace is mid 18C.

Although **Doughty House** was built in the 18C its front was remodelled in 1915 for Francis Cook. A rear extension housed his large collection of old master paintings, since dispersed. The house is now divided into flats.

•● *First R Nightingale Lane. Proceed to the Petersham Hotel.*

Location 21	**THE PETERSHAM HOTEL** *Giles 1865*
Nightingale Lane	The Petersham Hotel was built on the site of Sir Charles Nightingale's early-19C mansion, Nightingale Hall. Originally the hotel was called the Richmond Hill Hotel but changed its name to the Star and Garter Hotel in 1924 and adopted its present name in 1978.

It is believed to possess the largest unsupported staircase in England.

•● *Return to Richmond Hill R. On the corner R is The Wick.*

Location 22	**THE WICK** *Mylne 1775*
Richmond Hill	The house, little altered, was built for Lady St Aubyn on the site of the Bull's Head inn. It was for many years the home of the actor Sir John Mills and his family.

Location 23	**WICK HOUSE** *Chambers 1772*
Richmond Hill	Sir Joshua Reynolds built this as his weekend residence. It was remodelled in the late 19C and again, internally, in 1950 to provide residential accommodation for nurses at the Royal Star and Garter Home.

•● *Cross the road to the Richmond Hill Hotel opposite.*

32 Richmond

Location 24	**RICHMOND HILL HOTEL**
Richmond Hill	The hotel consists of 18C houses linked by later extensions. Its core is the recently renovated red brick building R. This was built *c.*1725 for the Countess of Mansfield.
	Wings were added on either side in the mid 19C and in 1875 the building became the Queen's Hotel.
	Buildings west of this are mainly mid 18C, some with Regency additions.
	An unfortunate extension, L of the ballroom entrance, is modern.
	The hotel adopted its present name just before the First World War.
	•● *Continue southward.*
Location 25	**RICHMOND GATE HOTEL**
Richmond Hill	Two cottages built in 1728, and two larger residences *c.*1784 were converted in the 1930s to form the Moorshead Hotel. It was extended to the rear and renamed in 1974.
	•● *Cross Richmond Hill and proceed to the Royal Star and Garter Home.*
Location 26	**THE ROYAL STAR AND GARTER HOME** *Cooper 1924*
Richmond Hill	This enormous edifice was constructed as a home and hospital for two hundred disabled war veterans. Most of the present residents fought in the Second World War. It was built on the site of the fashionable Star and Garter inn which stood from 1732 until it burnt down in 1870. A Victorian replacement proved to be too large and uneconomical. During the First World War disabled servicemen had been lodged there, but the building was demolished and replaced by the present structure.
	The home is not directly associated with the British Legion's poppy factory which stands at the base of the hill in Petersham Road.
	•● *Exit R. Cross Richmond Hill.*
	Immediately L is Ancaster House.
Location 27	**ANCASTER HOUSE** *R. Adam (?) 1772*
Queen's Road	Queen Charlotte granted the property, then within Richmond Park, to Peregrine, Duke of Ancaster. It had been the site of a hunting lodge. The house is now the official residence of the Commandant of the Royal Star and Garter Home.
	•● *Enter Richmond Park through the gate and cross the road to the entrance lodge.*
	The gate and its adjoining lodge were designed by *Capability Brown* in 1798.
	•● *Proceed through the park following the footpath R of the lodge.*

Richmond 33

| Location 28 | **RICHMOND PARK** |

Always open to pedestrians.

Open to motorists from dawn to dusk.

This 2000-acre royal park was once a royal hunting chase. Charles I purchased additional common land, walled in the area and named the enclosure New Park in 1637. Public access was for long permitted, but in the 18C, Prime Minister Sir Robert Walpole became Ranger, and only allowed token holders to enter. Admittance became even more restricted under the rangership of George II's daughter, Princess Amelia. Eventually, an outcry led to the reassertion of the public's rights and the gates were reopened.

Richmond Park is encircled, anti-clockwise from the north, by Richmond, East Sheen, Roehampton, Putney Vale, Coombe, Kingston, Ham and Petersham. Red and fallow deer roam the park freely; they can be dangerous if approached too closely when with their young.

The park is mainly flat and thinly wooded; it is at its most picturesque around the central Pen Ponds and in the Isabella Plantation, towards Kingston, where, in May, there is a famous display of azaleas and rhododendrons. There are only a few buildings within the park.

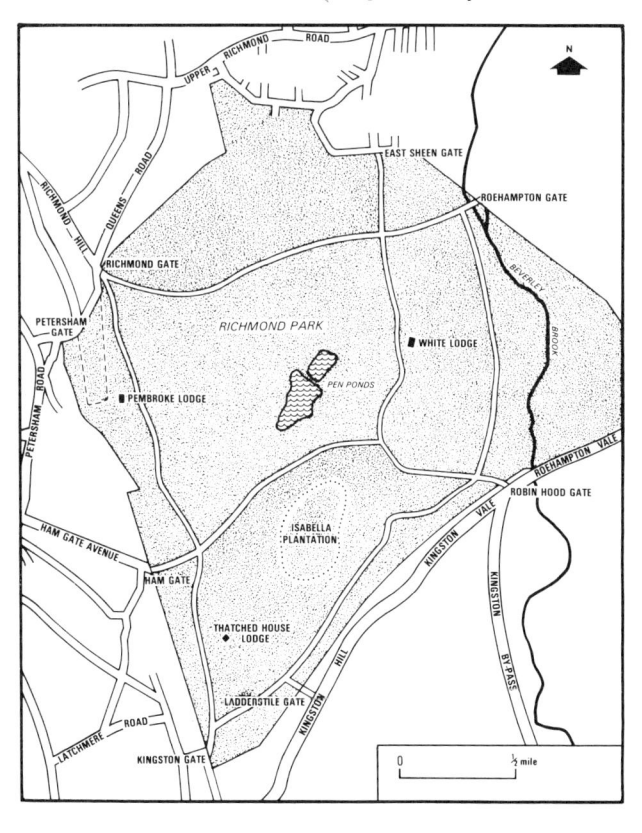

White Lodge. Built for George I by *Morris* in 1729 this was the birthplace of Edward VIII (later the Duke of Windsor). It now accommodates the Royal Ballet School.

The lodge is an early example of the Palladian revival.

Pavilions were added by *S. Wright* in 1752.

Thatched House Lodge *Kent* (?) *c.*1727. The residence of Princess Alexandra. This was built for Prime Minister Robert Walpole and was named from the thatched summerhouse that stands in the garden.

A car is necessary to explore the park fully, but a short walk to Petersham Gate gives a representative impression.

● From Richmond Gate take the path R, parallel with the road, following the west edge of the park. Enter the first gate R and follow the path ahead to Pembroke Lodge.

Pembroke Lodge. Built in the mid 18C and once the home of philosopher Bertrand Russell, it is now a municipal tea house.

● Descend the steps from the centre of the terrace that runs west of the house. The path R leads to a small gate. Descend the hill. The path R leads to Petersham Gate. Exit from Richmond Park and cross Petersham Rd. Take bus 65 to Richmond Station (BR) and District Line.

● Alternatively, if continuing to Ham and Petersham exit L Petersham Rd. Cross the road. The second path R leads to St Peter's Church.

Kew

Kew is, of course, mainly visited for its famous botanical gardens, still the most extensive in the world. However, due to its royal connections since the early 18C, many outstanding properties line its green and the north section of Kew Road. Within Kew Gardens, the smallest of England's royal palaces may be visited.

Timing Obviously, late spring and early summer are most spectacular at Kew Gardens but something of interest is always on view due to the extensive range of hot-houses that have been built. Kew Palace, within the gardens, can only be visited from April to September.

36 Kew

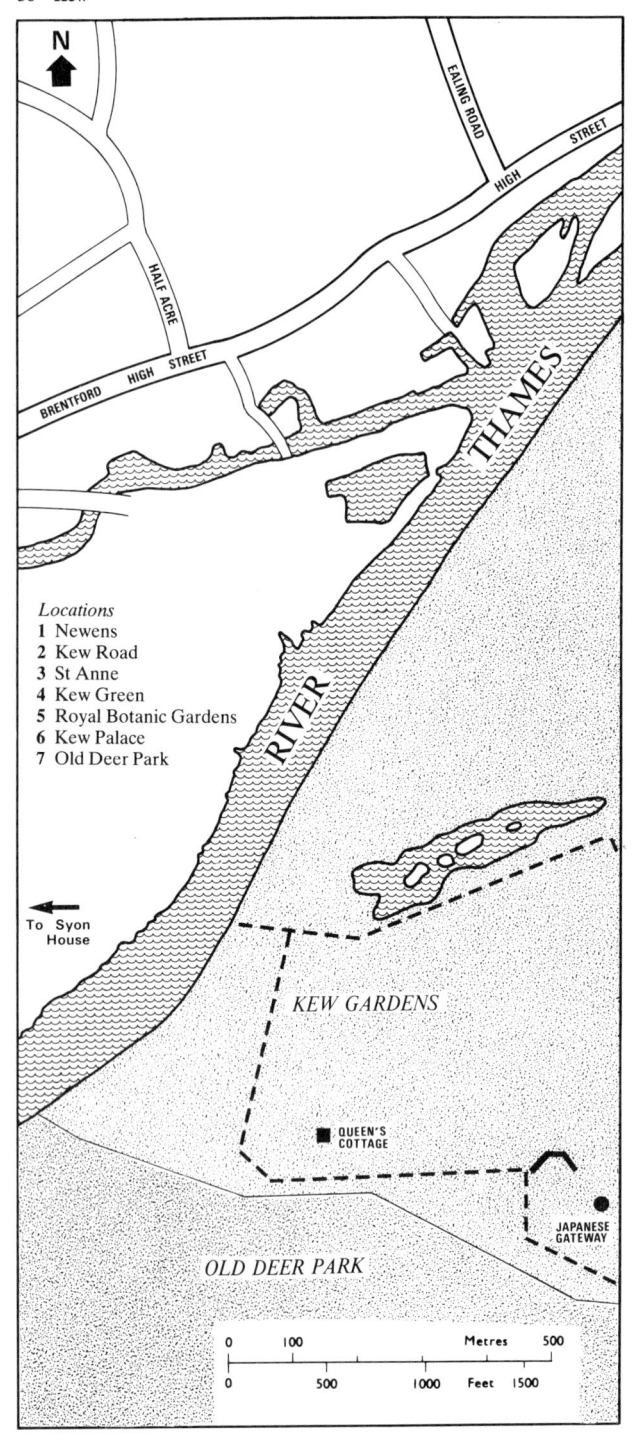

Locations
1 Newens
2 Kew Road
3 St Anne
4 Kew Green
5 Royal Botanic Gardens
6 Kew Palace
7 Old Deer Park

Kew 37

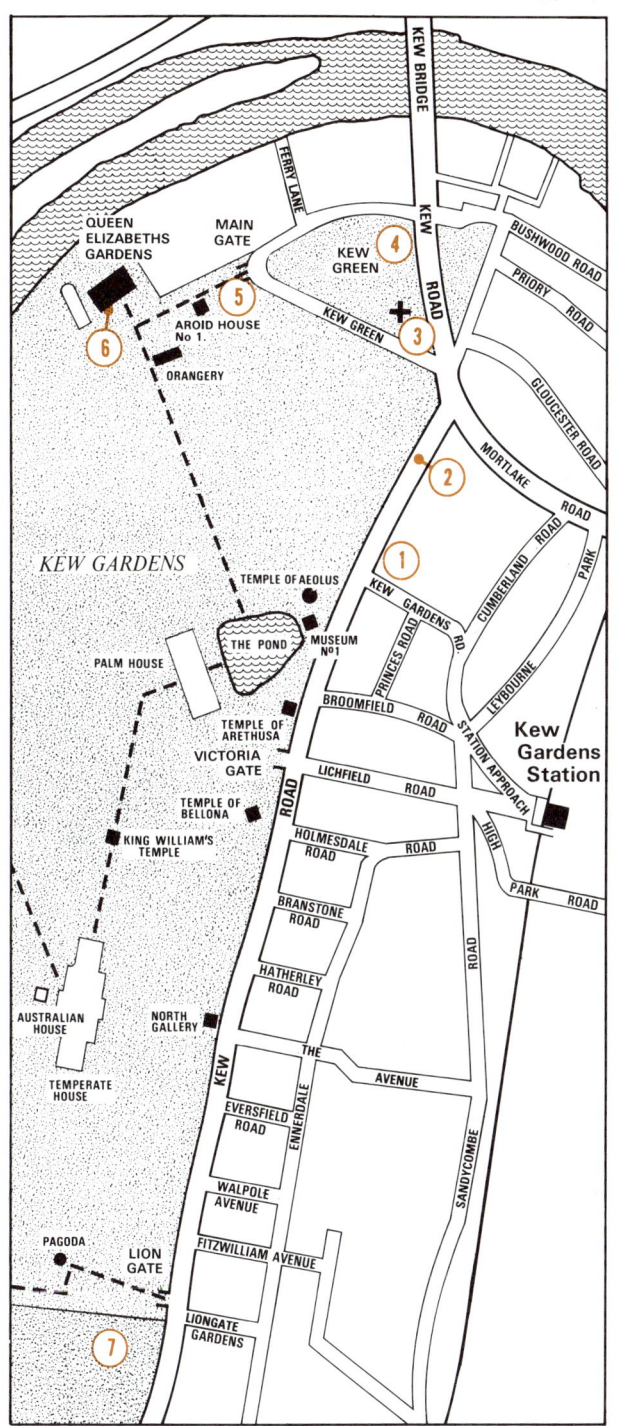

38 Kew

Start *From Kew Gardens Station, District Line, pass beneath the railway line by subway and exit from the station. Ahead Station Parade. First R Station Approach leads to Kew Gardens Rd. Second R Kew Road.*

Alternatively, boat from Westminster Pier, Easter–September. NB: the earliest arrival time is 12.00. From the landing stage proceed ahead to Kew Green. Continue to the south-west side (Location 4).

Location 1	**NEWENS**
288 Kew Road *Open Tuesday–Saturday, also Monday a.m.*	This traditional English tea shop is famed for its 'Maids of Honour' tarts. Reputedly, Henry VIII saw the queen's maids of honour eating them; the King tried one and was so impressed that he decreed that henceforth they should be cooked only for the Royal Family. After Henry's death, the recipe was sold for £1000 to a Mr Billett whose chef was an ancestor of the Newens family, the present owners of the shop. 'Maids of Honour' may be eaten within or bought to take away. •● *Exit R.*

Location 2	**KEW ROAD**
	The northern end of the road, towards Kew Green, has the properties of greatest interest. Further south, late Victorian villas and undistinguished blocks of modern flats predominate. Period houses are passed as follows: **No 294**, with a Regency bow window. **Nos 300–302**, Cumberland Place, dated 1831. **Nos 338–342**, Hanover Place, *c.*1712. **No 350**, early 18C with a Regency balcony. **No 352**, **Adam House**, late 18C with an Adam-style doorcase. **Nos 356** and **358**, **Denmark House**, both early 18C. •● *Cross Kew Rd. First L Kew Green. Proceed to St Anne's which stands in the green.*

Location 3	**ST ANNE** *1714*
Kew Green *Open afternoons in summer.*	The church originated as a simple chapel and replaced an early Tudor structure. Its nave was lengthened, and the north aisle added, by *J. J. Kirby*, a friend of the painter Gainsborough, in 1768. A south aisle and the west façade, altered by *Wyatville* in 1838, were added in 1805. The east end of the church, including the cupola, was rebuilt by *Stock* in 1884. Extending eastward from this is the mausoleum built for the Duke and Duchess of Cambridge by *Ferrey* in 1851. •● *Enter from the west portico.* The west gallery was added to accommodate George III's large family in 1805.

Kew 39

At the east end of the south aisle is the only impressive monument in the church, to Dorothy, Lady Dowager Capell, d.1721.

●▬ *Exit L.*

Buried in the churchyard are two famous painters. Gainsborough's tomb is L of the south porch and surrounded by railings.

Zoffany's tomb lies east of the church.

●▬ *Return to the south-east corner of Kew Green and proceed westward.*

Location 4	**KEW GREEN**

Kew began around this triangular village green which is now divided by the approach road to Kew Bridge. Its name derived from Kayhough – low lying land with a quay. Kew Green has been a fashionable address since the 16C. Cricket is played here on summer weekends.

Most of the houses on this side were built, or remodelled, in the 18C when the Royal Family returned to the area.

Nos 17–19, **Gamley Cottage**, is early 18C.

No 33, early 18C, set back from the road, was used as a study by the Earl of Bute.

No 37, **Cambridge Cottage**, early 18C, has a porch, added in 1840, which stretches half-way across the road. The house was the residence of the Duke of Cambridge, one of George III's many sons. Later occupants included the Earl of Bute and the mother of George V's consort, Queen Mary.

Nos 39–45, **The Gables**, is a 17C house remodelled in the 18C.

No 51, **Royal Cottage**, is late 18C.

●▬ *Pass Kew Gardens' gate and continue along the north side of Kew Green.*

Herbarium House consists of an 18C core, once known as Hunter House, and several extensions made between 1877 and 1969. Hunter House was the residence of another of George III's sons, the Duke of Cumberland, who later became King of Hanover, but was better known as 'Butcher Cumberland of Culloden'.

More 18C houses follow.

●▬ *Return eastward and enter Kew Gardens.*

Location 5	**ROYAL BOTANIC GARDENS (KEW GARDENS)**

Open 10.00–16.00. Admission charge. In summer the gardens close progressively later – up to 20.00 in July and August. Glass houses open 11.00–16.00 and also close later in summer

Inside the gates, by *Burton* 1846, an information board immediately L lists items of seasonal and special interest which may be seen. The gardens must be viewed selectively as they cover 288 acres and have no internal transport. Blooms are most spectacular in spring and early summer.

In the 18C the gardens were divided and formed the private grounds of three royal residences.

40 Kew

– up to 17.50. There is no additional charge.

Kew Palace and Kew House (the White House) stood to the north and Ormond Lodge (later Richmond Lodge) to the south, in what is now the Old Deer Park. The grounds were linked in 1802 although part of the Old Deer Park is once more a separate entity and serves as a golf course and athletic ground. Of the royal residences only Kew Palace survives.

Exotic trees and fruits were first planted here by Sir Henry Capell in the late 17C. Augusta, widow of Frederick, Prince of Wales, allocated an area for experiment in 1759, thus founding the botanic gardens. George III, 'Farmer George', enthusiastically continued this work. Queen Victoria presented Kew Gardens and its buildings to the nation in 1841.

The following suggested tour covers the items of greatest general interest.

•● *Proceed ahead.*

The first building passed R is the **Aroid House No 1.** This was one of a pair designed by *Nash* for Buckingham Palace and transferred here in 1836. The other survives *in situ*.

•● *Exit R and proceed ahead. Kew Palace lies R of the path.*

Location 6 | **KEW PALACE** *1631*

Kew Gardens

Open daily April–September 11.00–17.30. Admission charge.

Kew Palace was built on the site of the Earl of Dudley's Elizabethan house for Samuel Fortrey in 1631. Fortrey was a merchant of Dutch descent and named his residence the Dutch House. It was acquired by George II *c.*1728 and served as a nursery for his children. George IV, when Prince of Wales, and his brother Frederick lived and studied at the house in 1771.

Kew became the smallest royal palace in the country when George III and Queen Charlotte adopted the house as their temporary summer residence in 1802 following the demolition of the White House. Charlotte died here in 1818 and Kew Palace was never to be occupied again.

The house was designed in the Flemish style, fashionable during the Carolean period. Its brickwork is outstanding.

Above the door is the date 1631 and the initials of Samuel Fortrey, the builder of the house, and his wife Catherine.

Each window was originally divided into four lights by brick mullions and transoms but the usual conversion to sash took place in the 18C.

•● *Enter the palace. From the hall turn R to the King's Dining Room.*

Throughout Kew Palace, restoration work and furnishings emphasize its character during the early 19C occupancy of George III and Queen Charlotte. However, *Kent* had remodelled the interior *c.*1728 for its use as a royal nursery, and much of his décor survives.

King's Dining Room. William IV, when Duke of Clarence, held his wedding breakfast in this room. 'Jacobean' plasterwork, above the door ahead, is now believed to be an 18C imitation of the style, possibly by *Kent*.

King's Breakfast Room. Original panelling survives.

Staircase. This is carved in typical mid-18C style.

•● *Ascend to the first floor.*

The lantern R is 18C.

George III is depicted in needlework by *Mary Knowles* based on a contemporary painting by *Zoffany*.

•● *Enter the Queen's Boudoir and proceed clockwise.*

Queen's Boudoir. The ceiling's plasterwork is original and a late example of the Jacobean style.

Queen's Drawing Room. In this room, the Duke of Clarence, later William IV, and the Duke of Kent, both married German princesses on the same day in July 1818. Although now laid out as a music room, royal guests frequently played cards here.

The chimney-piece is original.

Anteroom. Wigs belonging to the king were kept in the closet in this room.

King's Bedchamber. The unusual chimney-piece was fitted in 1802 as part of the refurbishing of the house when it became a temporary royal residence.

George III used the dressing table.

Queen's Bedchamber. It is alleged that Queen Charlotte died sitting in the chair ahead R, on 17 November 1818.

•● *Proceed through the anteroom and descend the stairs.*

Page's Waiting Room. Exhibits include a large model for a royal palace by *Kent* intended to replace the White House but never built.

•● *Proceed through the library to the anteroom.*

Anteroom. Linenfold panelling is 16C work, retained from the Elizabethan house that previously stood on the site.

•● *Exit R and proceed to the south side of the palace and Queen Elizabeth's Gardens.*

The south façade is similar to the north façade.

Queen Elizabeth's Gardens. These gardens, laid out in formal 17C style, were opened by Elizabeth II in 1969.

•● *Exit and proceed ahead to the sundial.*

This late-17C sundial, erected by William IV in 1832, stands in the centre of the site previously occupied by Kew House, or the White House as it was later called. This was commissioned by

Frederick, Prince of Wales (who died after being struck by a cricket ball), and designed by *Kent* in 1735. It had replaced Sir Henry Capell's 17C residence which was separated from the Kew Palace estate by a road leading to Brentford Ferry. The White House was demolished in 1801. George III, an enthusiast of Gothic work, had commissioned *J. Wyatt* to build a new country mansion, overlooking the river behind Kew Palace. This was designed in the style of a medieval castle and known as the Castellated Palace. Its interiors, however, were never completed and the building was blown up by George IV in 1828.

•● *Turn L and continue ahead to the Orangery.*

Orangery *Chambers* 1757 (but dated 1761). This white stuccoed building is now used for temporary exhibitions and also serves as a bookshop.

•● *Exit and return to the west end of the Orangery. Turn L and follow the main path ahead to the pond.*

The tulips which bloom in May and June between the pond and the Palm House are outstanding.

On the opposite side, L of the pond, is **Museum No 1** by *Burton* 1857.

Ranged on the east side of the Palm House are the **Queen's Beasts**. They are stone replicas of plaster originals made by *James Woodford* in 1953 to front the Westminster Abbey annexe erected for the coronation of Elizabeth II.

Palm House *Burton* and *Richard Turner* (engineer) 1848. This iron and glass structure has been judged to be even more successful aesthetically than the old Crystal Palace which was built in 1851, also by *Decimus Burton*.

Within, a gallery above the palm tops is reached by spiral steps.

•● *Exit from the west side.*

Here is the famous rose garden that blooms June–September.

•● *Proceed southward to the flagstaff.*

Flagstaff. This is the trunk of a Douglas Fir tree, 225 ft high, which was brought from British Columbia and erected in 1959.

•● *Turn R and proceed westward.*

Temperate House *Burton* 1860. Known originally as the Winter Garden, this is judged to be less impressive than the same designer's Palm House.

The north and south wings were added in 1899.

During restoration in 1982 all the glazing was renewed and the wooden frames replaced by aluminium.

•● *Exit R and proceed in a north-west direction.*

Lake. Surrounded by weeping willow trees, the lake contains exotic wildfowl (which should not be fed).

● Follow the lakeside path, on either side, westward.

At the west end is a view of the main façade of Syon House on the north bank.

● Continue ahead towards the river and follow the path L. Take the first path L to the drinking fountain, then follow the path R to Queen's Cottage in the south-west of the gardens.

Open April–September Saturday, Sunday and Public Holidays 11.00–17.30. Admission charge.

Queen's Cottage. The cottage was a summer house built for Queen Charlotte in 1770 and allegedly designed by her. In May the bluebells that surround the cottage are in bloom. The property was presented to the nation by Queen Victoria in 1898.

Prints by *Hogarth* are exhibited in the central ground floor room.

A room upstairs has been painted to represent a floral arbour.

● Exit and return to the main path L. Take the first path R and the second path L. Proceed to the mound L.

Japanese Gateway. This is not a folly but a copy, four-fifths size, of a Buddhist temple gate known as Chokushi Mon – Gate of the Imperial Messenger. It was imported from Japan and first seen at the Japanese exhibition in 1910 before being presented to Kew.

● Proceed eastward to the pagoda which faces the Lion Gate exit.

Not open to the public.

Pagoda *Chambers* 1761. The 163 ft high pagoda was originally more decorative, with a total of eighty enamelled dragons protruding from the eaves which punctuate each storey. It is a survivor of the numerous mid-18C follies that once decorated the gardens. Most were the work of *Chambers* although he frequently used the designs of *Muntz*. Buildings lost include: a Moorish Alhambra, Turkish Mosque, Chinese House of Confucius, Gothic Cathedral, Theatre of Augustus and several Classical temples. Surviving elsewhere in the gardens, however, are three Classical temples and a ruined arch, all by *Chambers*, and King William's Temple, added by *Wyatville* in 1837 for William IV.

East of the pagoda, on the south side of the path, lies Old Deer Park.

Location 7   **OLD DEER PARK**

The park is shared by the Richmond Association Athletic Club and the Mid Surrey Golf Club. It was formerly the garden of Richmond Lodge which stood at its north end near the present Kew Gardens boundary.

Richmond Lodge was purchased by William III in the late 17C thus marking the first return of royalty to the area since Richmond Palace had been abandoned. William may have found it a convenient stopping-off point between his favourite residences at Kensington Palace and Hampton Court.

The Duke of Ormond leased the house *c.*1702, partly rebuilt it and renamed it Ormond Lodge. In 1719 the Prince of Wales acquired the property as a summer residence before moving to the White House. George III inherited both Ormond Lodge and the White House, and for a brief period their grounds, now Old Deer Park and Kew Gardens, were united. Ormond Lodge was demolished *c.*1775. Foundations were laid for a new royal palace but it was never built (a model for this by *Kent* is exhibited in Kew Palace). Garden buildings by *Kent*, including a Hermitage and Merlin's Cave, were demolished at the same time and the grounds laid out by *Capability Brown*.

•● *Leave Kew Gardens by the Lion Gate. Cross the road and take bus 27 or 65 to Richmond Station (BR) District Line.*

From the top of the bus, on the R side, can be viewed the old Kew Observatory which stands near the river in Old Deer Park (it is not open to visitors). This was built by *Chambers* in 1769 and had been commissioned, together with its great telescope, by George III for Herschel, the Astronomer Royal.

•● *Alternatively, if continuing to Richmond, cross The Quadrant immediately L. Take the footpath first R through the Oriel House archway. First L cross the railway bridge to Little Green (R).*

Ham and Petersham

Although close to London, Ham and Petersham are genuine villages with real fields grazed by real cows. Petersham, 'England's grandest village', is outstanding due to its quantity of great period mansions. Unfortunately, most of them line the main road from Richmond to Kingston which bisects the village. Escape riverwards brings some relief. North of Ham Common lies Ham House which is open to the public and uniquely retains most of its 17C décor and furnishings. This may, alternatively, be visited by ferry from Twickenham if preferred.

Timing Ham House does not open before 11.00 and closes Monday.

46 Ham and Petersham

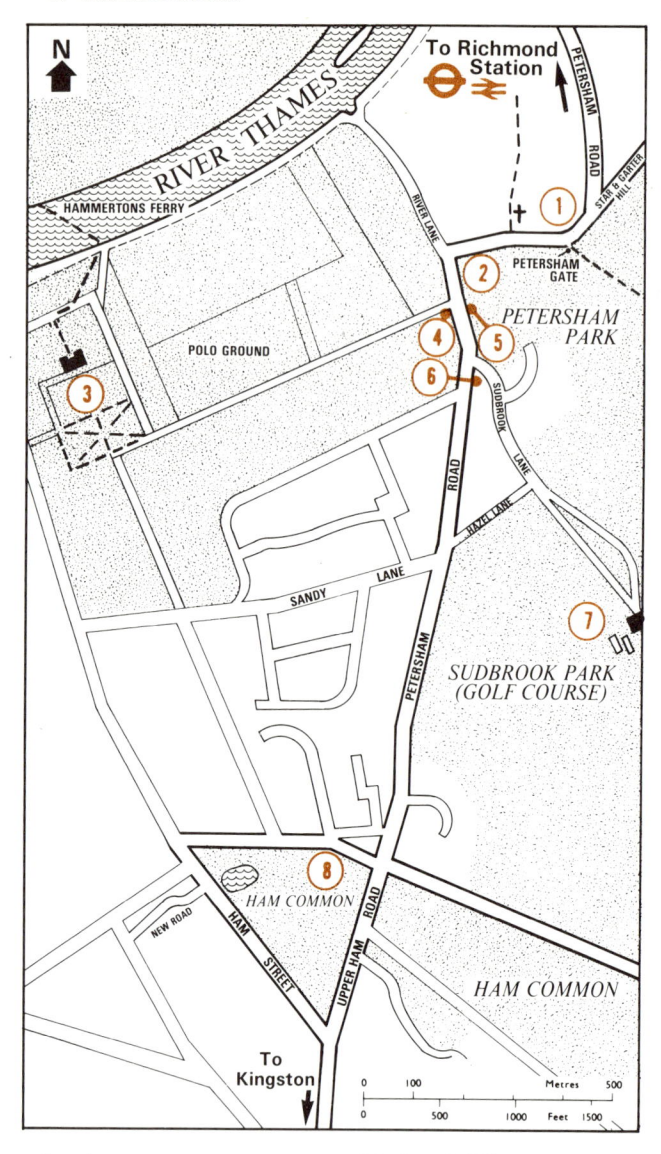

Locations
1 St Peter
2 Petersham Village
3 Ham House and Gardens
4 Ham House Gatehouse
5 Lodges of Old Petersham Park
6 Sudbrook Lane
7 Sudbrook Park
8 Ham Common

Start *Richmond Station, District Line or from Waterloo Station (BR). Exit from the station and take bus 65 or 71 southward to the Petersham Gate of Richmond Park (request stop). From the bus stop cross the road, turn L and continue southward passing the Dysart Arms.*

Alternatively, continue from Richmond as indicated on page 34.

Ham and Petersham 47

Noteworthy 18C houses passed R are **Park Gate** and **Church House**.

Follow the first path R to St Peter's Church. Ahead is the entrance to Church House. (The key to St Peter's may be obtained here if the church is locked.)

Location 1	**ST PETER**
Petersham Road	Although small, St Peter's, with its box pews and galleries, is a rare example of an English village church that retains its early 19C internal appearance.

The original Saxon church was rebuilt *c.*1266 and part of its chancel survives. George Vancouver, discoverer of Canada's Vancouver Island, is commemorated in the church and buried in the churchyard. The parents of Queen Elizabeth The Queen Mother, the Earl and Countess of Strathmore, were married at St Peter's in 1881.

The lower part of the **tower** was built in 1505 and the upper part in the 17C. Surmounting this is a lantern, added in 1790.

Immediately L of the tower is the **north transept**, built in the 17C, but with its upper part *c.*1790.

Much rebuilding took place following Second World War bomb damage.

•● *Proceed clockwise to the chancel that protrudes on the east side.*

The north wall of the **chancel** is 13C and retains the only lancet window (blocked) in the church.

The **south transept** was also built in the 17C but mostly rebuilt in 1840 when it was enlarged.

Some 17C brickwork remains at the base of the south transept's east wall.

Alongside the south wall, towards the east end of the churchyard, is the tomb of Captain George Vancouver.

•● *Continue to the west porch, built in 1840, and enter the church.*

Displayed, immediately R, is a beadle's uniform.

The short **nave**, rebuilt in 1805, is virtually the crossing of the church and does not extend west of the tower.

Immediately ahead is the font, dated 1740.

The west music gallery, above the entrance, was built in 1838. Other galleries were erected in 1840.

A beadle's staff is displayed L of the entrance.

North of this is George Vancouver's wall plaque, 1798.

The box pews are late-18C and rare surviving examples.

The pulpit, against the east wall of the north transept, was made in 1796.

Above the chancel arch are the arms of George III, acquired in 1810.

48 Ham and Petersham

Against the north wall of the **sanctuary** is the monument to George Cole, d.1624, and his wife and grandson.

Below the altar, in the Dysart vault, lies the Duchess of Lauderdale, 17C owner of nearby Ham House.

The reading desk, R of the chancel, is believed to be part of a late-18C three-decker pulpit.

●● *Return to Petersham Rd R. Remain on the west side.*

Location 2 — **PETERSHAM VILLAGE**

Petersham, with its outstanding period mansions, astonishingly remains a village, surrounded by fields and parkland, and has been described as England's grandest. Unfortunately, it is bisected by the main road between Richmond and Kingston, a daunting ribbon of noise, pollution and danger.

No 141, late 17C, retains rare examples of casement windows unconverted to sash.

No 143, **Petersham House**, *c.*1674, has an early-19C top storey and porch.

Opposite, on the east side, is **Montrose House** *c.*1670; for many years the residence of entertainer Tommy Steele. The house was enlarged and embellished early in the 18C.

Its main gates, on the corner ahead, are outstanding.

Rutland Lodge, on the west side, by *Jenner* (?) *c.*1660 was converted to flats following a fire in 1967. Its upper storey was added later, above the original carved eaves.

●● *First R River Lane. Cross to the south side.*

The **Manor House** is early-18C with a later porch.

Glen Cottage, next door, was occupied by George Vancouver from 1795 until his death in 1798.

Petersham Lodge, *c.*1740, has been remodelled and stuccoed.

●● *Continue ahead towards the river. Follow the path L to Ham House (Location 3) NB: sections of the path are impassable when there is a flood tide. Almost opposite the Hammerton Ferry landing stage, a short path L crosses a stream. Immediately R is a gap in the fence. The path leads to Ham House. It is important not to miss this, otherwise a detour of half a mile is necessary to reach the house from the west side.*

●● *Alternatively, if Ham House is not being visited, return to Petersham Road R and continue to Location 4.*

Location 3 — **HAM HOUSE AND GARDENS**

(940 1950)

The grounds are open daily 10.00–18.00. Admission free.

This Jacobean house, although much altered, retains, uniquely for the period, most of its original furnishings. The interior provides a greater insight into fashionable 17C life than any other house in the country.

Ham and Petersham   49

Ham House is open Tuesday–Sunday 11.00–17.00. Admission charge.

Ham House was built for Sir Thomas Vavasour in 1610 to an 'H' plan that followed the usual Elizabethan and Jacobean pattern. William Murray, Earl of Dysart, leased the house *c.*1626 and purchased the property in 1637. He then rearranged much of the interior. His daughter, Elizabeth, Countess of Dysart, married Sir Lyonel Tollemache *c.*1647 and inherited the house *c.*1654. After Tollemache's death Elizabeth married the Earl of Lauderdale, Charles II's Secretary of State for Scotland and they began major alterations in 1672.

The north front originally possessed a more vertical and picturesque appearance than it does now. There was a central bay above the doorway and the two existing three-storey loggias were surmounted by turrets with ogee (onion-shaped) caps and weather vanes in the manner of Charlton House near Greenwich. All this was removed by the Lauderdales, who preferred the then fashionable Classical style. To help achieve this, Classical busts were added to the forecourt walls.

Greater alterations were made on the south side (seen later) by the Lauderdales but the only major external alterations to Ham House after this were the rebuilding of the bays on both fronts and the usual conversion of most windows from casement to sash in the mid 18C.

The forecourt was originally enclosed by a north wall immediately fronted by a jetty. This wall was demolished *c.*1800 and its busts fixed to the north façade of the house.

The statue of a river god, in Coade stone, is based on a work by *Bacon c.*1784.

•● *Proceed anti-clockwise to view the south facade. Passed R are lodges and outbuildings.*

Wishing to increase their accommodation, the Lauderdales added a series of rooms on both floors between, and on either side of, the two south wings, *William Samwell*, 1674. This almost doubled the size of the house but, of course, destroyed the original 'H' plan.

The gardens of Ham House were laid out in the 17C and have been partly restored to their formal style.

•● *Return to the north façade and enter the house by the main door facing the forecourt.*

The initials of Sir Thomas Vavasour, and the date, 1610, are inscribed on the door.

As the house is operated by the Victoria and Albert Museum, which does not approve of labelling, every room will be named and its major contents described. Paintings are generally titled.

The house was privately owned by the Tollemache family until 1948 when it was presented, with its contents, to the nation and this unusual continuity of ownership, combined with a long period of storage, is why almost all of the furnishings original to the house survive. A few additional items of furniture have been provided by the V & A.

Much of the internal workmanship is Dutch, including some inset paintings by *Van de Velde, the Younger*.

Great Hall. When built, this formed the eastern half of the horizontal bar in the 'H' plan as, originally, there were no rooms on the south side. It was enlarged by Murray c.1637.

Most of the ceiling was removed in the late 17C to increase the height of the hall by combining it with the dining room above. The dining room ceiling of 1636 survived.

Windows in the south wall were filled when rooms were added south of the hall.

Carved figures of Mars and Minerva over the fireplace were allegedly modelled on Murray and his wife.

● Exit from the south-west corner.

Marble Dining Room. This was the first of the domestic rooms to be added by the Lauderdales. It was named 'Marble' from the original black and white marble floor which was replaced by the present decorative wooden floor in the mid 18C.

The wall covering is 17C gilt leather.

● Exit from the south-west corner.

Duke's Dining Room. The wall hangings are a reproduction of the 17C originals.

Duchess's Bedchamber. Originally, the Duke occupied this bedchamber but he later exchanged rooms with the Duchess.

The bed and its covers are modern reproductions of 18C originals.

Above the door are sea paintings by *Van de Velde the Younger*.

Duke's Closet. Damask wall coverings reproduce the 17C colour scheme.

● Return to the Marble Dining Room and exit from the south-east corner.

Withdrawing Room. Furnishings are c.1675.

● Exit from the south-east corner.

Yellow Bedchamber. This room, part of the original house, was Lady Dysart's bedchamber before the extension was built. It became Lord Lauderdale's bedchamber c.1677 when he exchanged with her.

● Exit from the south-west corner.

White Closet. The closet was retained by the Duchess after the exchange of bedchambers.

The ceiling painting is by *Verrio*.

Ham and Petersham 51

The Duchess's Private Closet. This closet was also retained by the Duchess following the exchange; the arrangement could hardly have been convenient.

•▶ Return to the Great Hall.

Chapel. Created in the north-east bay by the Lauderdales, the chapel retains its original rare altar hangings.

•▶ Exit ahead.

Inner Hall. Furniture displayed here is mid-18C.

Great Staircase. Added to the house for Murray, c.1637, the staircase has a balustrade of carved and pierced panels and is an early example of its type.

The ceiling's plasterwork is contemporary with the staircase.

•▶ Ascend to the top of the stairs L.

Lady Maynard's Chamber. The room was occupied by Lady Maynard, the Duchess's sister, from 1679 to 1682. The oak frieze is Jacobean reproduction, carved early in the 19C.

Most furniture is 19C.

•▶ Exit from the south-east corner.

Lady Maynard's Dressing Room. This was also occupied by Lady Maynard.

•▶ Return to Lady Maynard's Chamber and exit from the north side. Proceed ahead.

Museum Room. Originally a bedroom, textiles are displayed.

•▶ Exit from the south-west corner.

Cabinet of Miniatures. This was once a servants' room. Miniatures displayed include 'Elizabeth I' by *Hilliard*.

Exhibited in a case is a lock of hair allegedly cut from the Earl of Essex's head, immediately preceding his execution in 1601.

•▶ Exit from the south side.

Round Gallery. Before most of the floor was removed early in the 18C, this served as the Great Dining Room. It forms the first of the State Rooms which were created to impress important guests.

The ceiling and frieze were plastered for Murray c.1637.

Paintings are by *Cleyn, Kneller* and *Lely*.

•▶ Exit from the north-west corner.

North Drawing Room. The woodwork, plaster ceiling and frieze were made for Murray c.1637.

Its 17C armchairs retain their original silk covers.

Inset paintings are by *Cleyn*.

52 Ham and Petersham

→ Exit from the north side.

Green Closet. Miniature paintings were originally displayed here.

The modern reproduction wall hangings simulate the room's appearance after 1670.

The paintings on the ceiling and its cove are by *Cleyn*.

Long Gallery. This formed part of the original house but was redecorated for Murray in 1639.

Many of the portraits are by *Lely*.

→ Exit from the south-west corner.

Library Closet. Displayed are plans for a Whitehall Palace by *Inigo Jones* that never materialized.

Library. This, together with its closet, was added by the Lauderdales, thus extending Ham House to the west c.1674.

The library steps are c.1740.

→ Return to the Long Gallery. Exit ahead from the south-east corner.

Antechamber to the Queen's Bedchamber. This was one of the three rooms added between the south front wings by the Lauderdales. It was then known as the Green Drawing Room. The furniture is late 17C.

→ Exit from the south-east corner.

Queen's Bedchamber. The room was prepared for a visit by Catherine of Braganza, Charles II's consort. It was remodelled c.1740 and converted to a drawing room; tapestries were then hung.

Queen's Closet. Although small, this is the most sumptuous of all the rooms. Its oval ceiling panel was probably painted by *Verrio*.

The scagliola (imitation marble) fireplace is an early English example.

→ Return through the State Rooms to the Long Gallery. Exit from the west side to the Round Gallery and descend the stairs. Exit from Ham House and proceed through the north entrance gate. Follow the path R and turn R passing the east side of Ham House. The path bears L.

Passed L are the **Ham House Polo Grounds**.

The German School, **Deutsche Schule** designed by German architects in 1972, is passed next. It stands in the grounds of **Douglas House** c.1700, which overlooks the path further south.

The old stable block of the house follows (now part of the school).

→ Continue to the gatehouse ahead.

Location 4	**HAM HOUSE GATEHOUSE** *1898*
Petersham Road	The gatehouse was built, with due deference to the 17C Ham House, in mock Jacobean style. It is now divided into two private residences.

→ Cross Petersham Rd to Farm House opposite.

Ham and Petersham 53

Location 5	**LODGES OF OLD PETERSHAM PARK** *17C*
Petersham Road	**Farm House**, and **No 190** Petersham Road which faces it, are genuine early-17C buildings. The two properties were originally the lodges to Petersham Park (also called Petersham Lodge). Petersham Park was a mansion built in the 17C but rebuilt in the 18C by *Lord Burlington* for William Stanhope, first Viscount Petersham. The house was demolished early in the 19C and its extensive grounds incorporated with Richmond Park.
	●● *Turn R and proceed southward. Where Petersham Rd curves R continue ahead following Sudbrook Lane.*
Location 6	**SUDBROOK LANE**
	Sudbrook Cottage and **Box Cottage** on the east side are early 18C.
	Gort Lodge, opposite, is also early 18C. It was built as one residence with **Gort House** which lies behind, fronting Petersham Rd.
	Harrington Lodge was built c.1700.
	Mullion, opposite, is a Georgian residence.
	●● *Continue to the archway at the end of Sudbrook Lane and follow the path through the golf course to Sudbrook Park.*
Location 7	**SUDBROOK PARK** *Gibbs 1726*
Richmond Golf Club (940 1463)	The house, now the clubhouse of Richmond Golf Club, is a rare example of a private residence by *Gibbs*. It is basically designed to a Palladian plan but its detailing is Baroque.
Grudgingly open to visitors (although a statutory requirement) to view the Cube Room, one afternoon each month. Telephone to ascertain the date.	The main elevation has been completely altered by the later addition of a portico.
	●● *Enter the hall immediately. Directly behind this is the* **Cube Room.**
	The Cube Room is one of Gibbs's most Baroque interiors; few in the London area match its flamboyance.
	●● *Exit from the house and return to Sudbrook Lane. Immediately L is Hazel Lane. Continue to the end. L Petersham Rd. Take bus 65 southbound to Ham Common (north side) to avoid a ten minute walk of little interest. From the bus stop return northward. First L Ham Common north side.*
Location 8	**HAM COMMON**
	This triangular section surrounded by houses is often regarded as the extent of Ham Common; the common in fact continues eastward from the Petersham Road and that section is three times larger.
	The north and west sides of this triangular section are of greater architectural interest.
	Hardwick House is late 18C.

St Michael's Convent now occupies Orford Hall, an early-18C residence with later wings.

Two 17C **lodges**, now private houses, once flanked the south entrance to Ham House.

Selby House is 18C.

●● *Turn L and follow Ham Street which, for this stretch, forms the west side of Ham Common.*

Endsleigh Lodge, *c.*1800, has wings with typical Adamesque fans above their windows.

Little House and, after New Road, **Glebe Cottage** and **Gordon House** are 18C.

Forbes House is a good Georgian fake, built in 1936.

Langham House is 18C.

Cassel Hospital now occupies Cassel House, built in the early 19C.

●● *At Upper Ham Rd turn L and take bus 65 northward to Richmond Station (BR), District Line.*

Twickenham

Old Twickenham, bordering the Thames, retains the most nautical feel of all London's riverside villages. Many of its great 18C mansions survive and some may be entered. Although spoilt by small, indiscreetly placed car parks, much of the ancient core of Twickenham, huddled around Church Street, survives. Horace Walpole's house, Strawberry Hill, that inspired the Neo-Gothic style, is well preserved and may be visited, albeit with limitations. Ham House, described in this book as part of the visit to Ham and Petersham may, alternatively, be included in a visit to Twickenham if preferred.

Timing Fine weather is essential. Orleans House does not open until 13.00 and closes Monday. Marble Hill House closes Friday. Ham House, if included, also closes Monday. The ferry from Twickenham to Ham House operates daily Easter–October and weekends only mid-November–Easter (depending on weather). The service is suspended between 13.00–14.00.

56 Twickenham

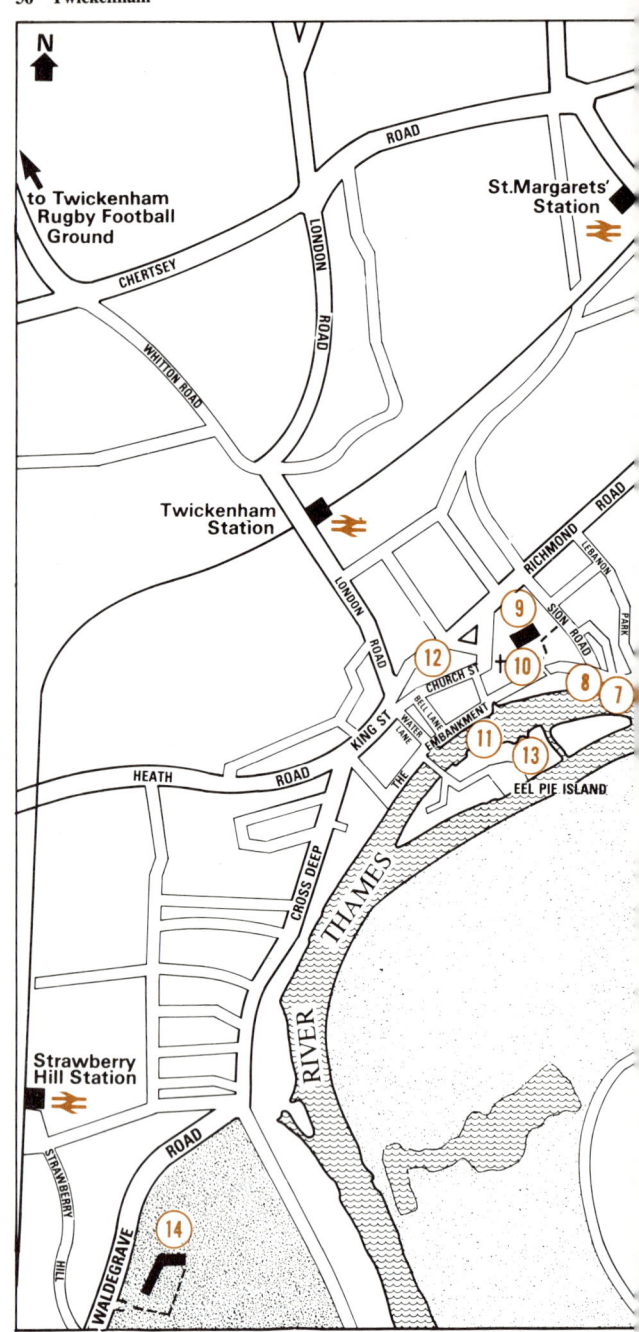

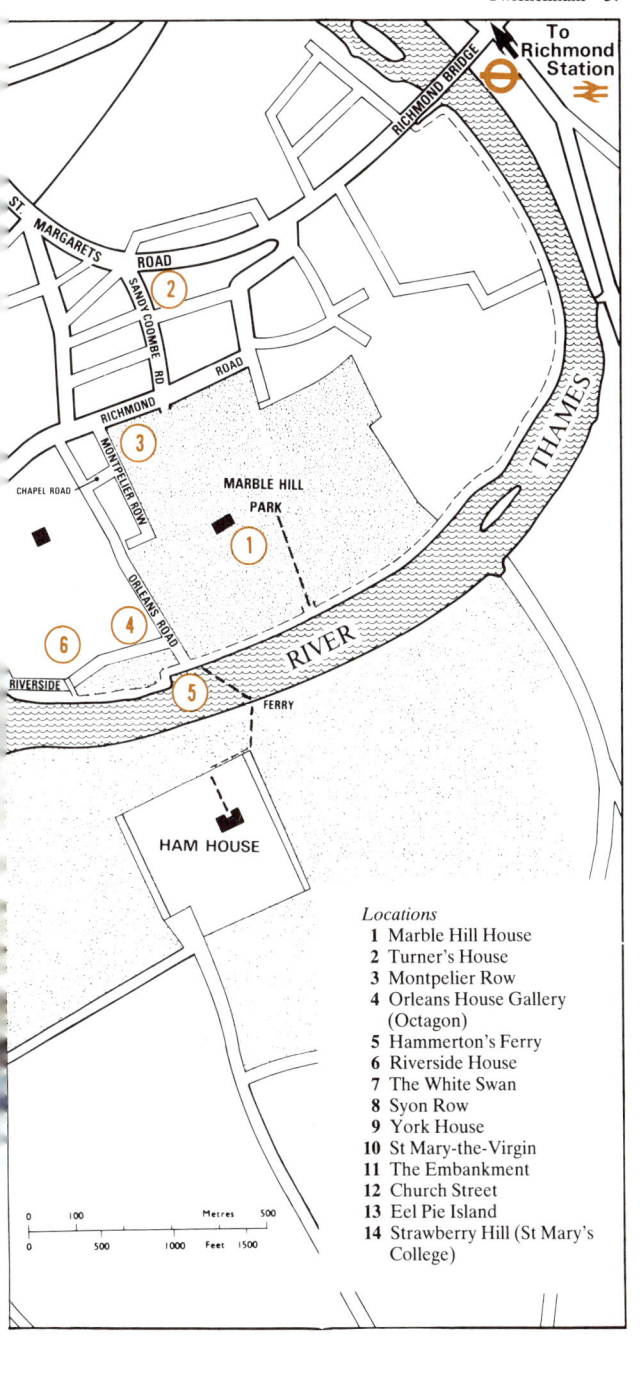

Twickenham 57

Locations
1 Marble Hill House
2 Turner's House
3 Montpelier Row
4 Orleans House Gallery (Octagon)
5 Hammerton's Ferry
6 Riverside House
7 The White Swan
8 Syon Row
9 York House
10 St Mary-the-Virgin
11 The Embankment
12 Church Street
13 Eel Pie Island
14 Strawberry Hill (St Mary's College)

58 Twickenham

Start *Richmond Station, District Line or from Waterloo Station (BR). Exit from the station L and proceed ahead to Richmond Bridge. Cross the bridge and descend the steps L to the towpath R. Proceed towards the gate R to Marble Hill Park. Enter the grounds and continue ahead to the house which lies in the west part of the grounds.*

Alternatively, Twickenham may be approached by river, Easter–September, from Westminster Pier (930 2062) to Richmond Pier. Cross Richmond Bridge and continue as indicated above. The earliest boat (10.30) arrives at 13.00, too late to complete the itinerary if Strawberry Hill is to be seen. If a river trip is preferred it is better to return to London by boat from Richmond, but check the time of the last boat (940 2244).

Location 1	**MARBLE HILL HOUSE** *1729*

Marble Hill Park
(892 5115)

Open Saturday–Thursday 10.00–17.00. Sunday 14.00–17.00. Closes 16.00 November–January. Admission free.

The grounds are now rather different from those designed by *Alexander Pope* and laid out by *Bridgeman* when the house was built. Marble Hill House was commissioned for Henrietta Howard, later Countess of Suffolk. She was a Maid of Honour to Caroline, Princess of Wales, and the house was paid for by Henrietta's 'close friend' the Prince of Wales, later George II. It was built by *Roger Morris*, to a design by *Colen Campbell*, based on original sketches by *Henry Herbert*. Mrs Fitzherbert occupied the house in 1795. Restoration was completed in 1966.

The building, which played an important part in the Palladian revival, is stuccoed and painted cream with stone dressings.

● *Enter from the north door.*

The furnishings throughout are contemporary with, although not from, the house.

● *Ascend the stairs R to the first floor.*

The Great Room. This takes the form of a 24 ft cube and was influenced by the work of Inigo Jones.

The carving is by *James Richards*.

Displayed are copies of paintings by *Van Dyck*.

● *Turn L.*

The Countess's Bedchamber. The Thames-side painting is by *Richard Wilson*.

The 18C chimney-piece was brought from elsewhere.

● *The cantilevered stairs lead to the second floor. When convenient, staff will show the rooms to visitors.*

Green Room and **Wrought Room.** These were redecorated in 1985.

● *Descend to the ground floor.*

On the south side is the central hall.

● *Proceed L to the Breakfast Parlour.*

Breakfast Parlour. This retains its screen by *Herbert* which was possibly based on designs by *Inigo Jones*.

Dining Parlour. This room was created by

Twickenham 59

Brettingham in 1751, by combining two small rooms.

●▶ Exit from the house L and proceed to the west side of the park.

Stables. These ivy-clad, early-19C buildings have been converted to tea rooms.

The clock was fitted in 1830.

●▶ Proceed northward across the lawns and exit from the grounds. Cross Richmond Rd immediately and continue ahead to Sandycombe Rd. Proceed to the end. R Turner's house.

Location 2	**TURNER'S HOUSE** *J. M. W. Turner 1814*
Sandycombe Lodge, Sandycombe Road	This white, Italian-style house at the far end of Sandycombe Road, partly hidden by trees, was initially built as a country retreat for the great painter J. M. W. Turner; subsequently, his father lived here in retirement. It is *Turner*'s only known architectural work. *●▶ Return to Richmond Rd R. First L Montpelier Row.*
Location 3	**MONTPELIER ROW** *c.1724*
	Montpelier Row has been judged outer London's finest early-Georgian terrace. Two famous poets lived here, Tennyson at No 15 and Walter de la Mare at No 30. **Nos 1–15** were built as a speculative development, their exteriors are similar apart from the door surrounds. Towards the end R, following the Victorian additions, is **No 25**, designed for himself by architect *Geoffrey Darke* in 1967. *●▶ Return northward. First L Chapel Rd. L Orleans Rd. Enter Orleans Park R. The path R leads to Orleans House (Location 4).* *●▶ Alternatively, if Ham House is to be visited from Twickenham, bear in mind that Orleans House does not open until 13.00 and it may, therefore, be preferable to visit Ham House at this stage. If so, continue to the end of Orleans Rd. Proceed through the gate L. Ahead Warren Footpath. Hammerton's Ferry (Location 5) to Ham House leaves from the jetty R. Return later to see Orleans House.*
Location 4	**ORLEANS HOUSE GALLERY (OCTAGON)** *Gibbs 1720*
Orleans Park (892 0221) *Gardens open daily 09.00–sunset. House open Tuesday Saturday 13.00–17.30. Sunday 14.00–17.30. Closes 16.30 October– March. Admission free.*	Orleans House was built for James Johnston, William III's Secretary of State for Scotland, by *John James* in 1692. It lay east of the existing gallery but was demolished by its owner, the shipping magnate William Cunard, in 1927. 'Orleans' was adopted for the name of the house following the residency of Louis-Philippe, Duc d'Orleans, from 1800 to 1817. Don Carlos of Spain also lived here in 1876. The gallery was added to the house by *Gibbs* in

1720, probably to accommodate a reception for Princess Caroline. Mrs Ionides bequeathed the estate to the local authority in 1962.

The octagonal design of the gallery was influenced by pavilions that were fashionable in the gardens of great German houses in the early 18C.

Urns originally stood on the pilasters above parapet level.

•● *Enter the gallery*.

The Baroque plasterwork is by the Italians *Artari* and *Bagutti*, whom Gibbs employed for most of his major work.

Busts of Queen Caroline and George II are displayed.

Two of the medallions probably also represent the King and Queen, with the third possibly depicting Louis-Philippe.

Topographical paintings of the area are displayed in the adjoining south-west wing which was built to link the gallery with the house.

•● *Exit and return to Riverside R. Continue ahead to Riverside House (Location 6) on the corner.*

•● *Alternatively, continue to Hammerton's Ferry and proceed to Ham House.*

Location 5	**HAMMERTON'S FERRY**
Jetty off Warren Footpath (892 9620) *Operates daily Easter–October. Mid November–Easter Saturday and Sunday only. No service between 13.00–14.00.*	This, one of the few private ferries still operating on the Thames, is generally reliable but telephone first to confirm that it is operating. Hail the ferryman when he is on the opposite bank. Ask him to point out the concealed east entrance to Ham House grounds to avoid an unnecessary walk. If visiting Strawberry Hill later, book the return with the ferryman before 13.00.

Location 6	**RIVERSIDE HOUSE** *c.1810*
Riverside	This is, after York House, Twickenham's largest house in the Classical style. Riverside House possesses typical Regency bow windows but is difficult to see as it lies behind a high wall.

•● *Continue ahead*.

Passed R are **Ferry House**, late 18C, and **Ferryside**, also 18C but now roughcast.

Location 7	**THE WHITE SWAN** *18C*
Riverside	Known to locals as 'The Dirty Duck', the pub possesses a first floor terrace and a riverside garden separated from the building by the road. Balconies were added in the early 19C.

•● *Exit R.*

Three houses with Regency fronts are passed.

Twickenham 61

Location 8	**SYON ROW** *1721*
Sion Road	Twelve houses make up this terrace (note the original spelling of 'SION' on the plaque). They were built only three years before Montpelier Row nearby (Location 3) but their overhanging eaves, breaking the 1707 Building Act, give them an earlier appearance. However, it is possible that work on the Row began earlier.
	●● *Continue ahead. Proceed through the gate to York House L.*

Location 9	**YORK HOUSE** *c.1650 (?)*
Richmond Road (892 0032) *The house is only open for guided tours during 'Twickenham Week' at the end of May. The gardens are open daily. Admission free.*	An old farmhouse, Yorke Farm, was replaced by the present house which retained the name. The mansion is believed to have been built by the Earl of Manchester. It became the summer residence of the Earl of Clarendon, Lord Chancellor to Charles II, in the late 17C. Allegedly, the house was occupied by James II when Duke of York; his first wife, Anne Hyde, was Clarendon's daughter. Like Orleans House nearby, York House was favoured as a residence by members of the French Royal Family early in the 19C. The last private owner was an Indian tycoon, Sir Ratan Tata, who installed the elaborate garden statuary. It now accommodates local authority offices.
	York House was remodelled early in the 18C and most of the external detailing dates from this period.
	Internally, only a mid-17C staircase in the north wing is of particular interest.
	●● *Proceed L through the gardens to the rock garden on the south side with its pool and palm tree. Cross the ornate bridge ahead R.*
	In the south-west corner of the grounds is an amusingly vulgar fountain (1904) with nude Italianate maidens.
	●● *Follow the river path R to the exit. L Riverside.*
	Passed R is **Dial House** (the vicarage) 1890. In its grounds is a sundial made in 1726 for a now demolished 18C Twickenham mansion designed by *James*, the architect of the parish church.
	●● *First R Church Lane leads to Church St R and St Mary's.*

Location 10	**ST MARY-THE-VIRGIN** *James c.1714*
Church Street (891 5446) *Open infrequently apart from services.*	The earliest record of a church on the site is in 1332. St Mary's was rebuilt of Kentish ragstone towards the end of the 14C but its nave collapsed in 1713. This was rebuilt in brick by *James*, but the ancient tower was retained.
	Externally, the fine quality of the brickwork is apparent.
	●● *Enter from the north door.*
	Renovations in 1860 removed the box pews but the galleries, although altered, were retained.

The ceiling of the church and the sanctuary have recently been redesigned by *Richardson*.

The **north aisle**'s east window commemorates painter Sir Godfrey Kneller who is buried in the church. His monument, intended for St Mary's, is in Westminster Abbey.

Although the pulpit was made in 1714 its tester is modern.

In front of the chancel step L, a brass floor plate commemorates the burial in the church of the poet Alexander Pope, d.1744. The plate was presented by three American scholars. Pope lived nearby at Pope's Villa in Cross Deep, since demolished.

He lies beneath the adjoining stone inscribed with a 'P'.

The altar rails and reredos are original.

In the **sanctuary** is the monument to Sir W. Humble, d.1680, and his son, by *Bird* (?). This was brought from the earlier church.

On the east wall of the **south aisle**, beneath the gallery, a monument, also from the earlier church, commemorates Francis Poulton, d.1642, and his wife.

●● *Return to the west end of the church.*

Beneath the **tower** are two 17C monuments: Sir Joseph Ashe, from the studio of *Gibbons*; and General Lord Berkeley of Stratton.

●● *Proceed L to the door in the south-west corner. A further door L leads to the south gallery. Unfortunately, this will be locked unless there is an attendant present.*

The monument to George and Anne Gostling is by *Bacon the Younger*, 1800.

Nathaniel Piggott, d.1737, is commemorated by a monument designed by *Scheemakers*.

●● *Proceed to the door in the north-west corner. A further door R leads to the north gallery – again probably locked.*

The monument to Admiral Sir Chaloner Ogle is by *Rysbrack*, 1751.

Alexander Pope is commemorated by a memorial commissioned by his friend Bishop Warburton in 1761.

At the east end, a further memorial to Alexander Pope commemorates, not the poet, but his father and mother; it is by *Bird*.

Below this is a memorial to author Richard Owen Cambridge, d.1802.

●● *Exit from the church L. First L Church Lane. Second R The Embankment.*

Passed R is **The Riverside Tavern**, *c.*1720.

Twickenham 63

Location 11	**THE EMBANKMENT**
	A passage separates the houses along The Embankment from their original riverside gardens – now car parks.

No 2 is early 18C.
No 3, **Strand House**, in Queen Anne style, is probably earlier.
No 5 appears to be the oldest building. Its timber frame indicates the early 17C (?).

At the end, R, the Mission Hall by *Edis*, 1871, has been converted to form the **Mary Wallace Theatre**.

•● *First L Church Lane. L Church St.* |

Location 12	**CHURCH STREET**
	This, the original village high street, is basically 18C and has been recently restored after years of neglect. At the north end, 18C cottages were demolished in the 1950s and their sites have unfortunately become car parks.

•● *First L Bell Lane. R The Embankment. Cross the pedestrian bridge to Eel Pie Island.* |

Location 13	**EEL PIE ISLAND**
	There is no road access, nor is the island linked with the opposite bank. The two main paths may be walked along in spite of 'Private' notices; both are cul de sacs. A hotel on the south side, now demolished to make way for housing, once sold eel pies to trippers – hence the name. Leafy alleyways link the various styles of dwelling; wooden chalets predominate.

•● *Follow the main path ahead.*

Hurley Cottage R is judged to be the island's most picturesque building.

•● *Return and take the second path L just before the bridge. Return from this and cross the bridge to The Embankment R. First L Water Lane leads to King St L.*

•● *If visiting Strawberry Hill, take bus 33 to St Mary's College. From the bus stop continue northward to the porter's lodge L.*

•● *Alternatively, if not visiting Strawberry Hill, cross King St and take bus 33, 90B or 290 to Richmond Station (BR), District Line.* |

Location 14	**STRAWBERRY HILL (ST MARY'S COLLEGE)**
Waldegrave Road (892 0051)

Open Wednesday and Saturday 14.30 by appointment only. Apply to the Principal Closed during term holidays at Christmas, Easter and mid-June–mid-October. Admission free. | Wealthy Horace Walpole, writer, dilettante and younger son of Prime Minister Sir Robert Walpole, leased a late-17C cottage at Strawberry Hill Shot in 1747 and purchased the estate two years later. Deciding it was too small for adaptation to Classical grandeur he transformed it in the Gothic style.

Although seeking to achieve a playful Gothic fantasy, Walpole insisted, for the first time, that the Gothic detailing should be reasonably accurate. *William Robinson* began the alterations in 1748, but his work was not regarded as Gothic |

64 Twickenham

enough and Walpole set up a 'committee on taste' to complete the work. This committee, made up from his personal friends, included *John Chute*, *Richard Bentley*, *Thomas Pitt* and the poet *Thomas Gray*. *Robert Adam* joined them later. To ensure authenticity, examples of Gothic design from great north European churches were copied. There was no objection, however, to a tomb becoming a fireplace or window tracery a ceiling. The house was ready by 1766, but Walpole's work was not finished until 1776 when the Beauclerk Turret was built.

Strawberry Hill was so influential in promoting the 18C Neo-Gothic style (as opposed to the 19C Gothic Revival) that this is often referred to as 'Strawberry Hill Gothic'.

In the 19C, Strawberry Hill was neglected until Lady Waldegrave inherited the property and restored it in 1856. It is now a College of Further Education.

•● *Proceed with the guide to view the south façade.*

Immediately R, divided by a bay, is the original small house of 1698. Its south front was remodelled by *Chute* in 1752. The bay itself may have been an addition.

West of this is the **Long Gallery** by *Chute*, 1762.

In the 19C, Tudor-style chimneys replaced the original pinnacles and the towers were lengthened.

Pebbledash, added at a later stage, unfortunately replaced the earlier roughcast rendering.

The bay was recently heightened by one storey by *Richardson*.

Immediately L of the Long Gallery, running northward, is the wing added in 1862 on the site of Walpole's stables. It is believed that *Lady Waldegrave* designed the building herself.

South of this is the office wing designed by *James Essex* in 1779 but built under the direction of *Wyatt* in 1790. This was Walpole's 'Dairy and Coal Hole'.

Other buildings to the south, except for the Chapel in the Wood, described later, were built in the 20C.

The grounds of Strawberry Hill originally led eastward to the river, and views of the Thames were unobstructed by trees. Sheep grazed around the house adding to the rural ambience. Although the site of the house is raised slightly above river level, Walpole was certainly exaggerating when he christened it Strawberry Hill.

•● *Entered immediately is the Little Parlour.*

It is known that Walpole preferred soft lighting and muted colours and much of the décor of the house would have been more sombre than it is today. Unfortunately, all of Walpole's furniture was disposed of in the 'Great Sale' of 1842. Some of it may be seen in the Lewis Walpole Library at Farmington, Connecticut, USA.

Walpole's unusual collection of antiquities was also dispersed at this sale. A contemporary jested that Walpole would have purchased 'the wart from Cromwell's nose, had it been available'.

Set in windows throughout the house are fragments of ancient stained glass. Most of it is 17C and several pieces are Dutch.

Little Parlour. Much of Walpole's collection was displayed here.

The chimney-piece by *Bentley*, 1753, was inspired by Bishop Ruthall's tomb in Westminster Abbey.

Visitors are usually shown rooms in the following order but changes may be made from time to time.

Walpole's Yellow Bedroom. This is sometimes called the 'Beauty Room' as reproductions of 'The Windsor Beauties' by *Lely* were hung here.

The chimney-piece, by *Bentley*, was originally painted black and yellow.

Staircase Hall. Formed by *Bentley* in 1754, the balustrade's tracery is believed to have been inspired by work at Rouen Cathedral.

Lancet windows are post-war additions by *Richardson*.

Little Cloister. Built by *Chute* in 1761. Its Oratory was added in 1762.

Great Parlour or **Refectory**. Completed in 1754, the chimney-piece is by *Bentley*.

The window was enlarged in 1774.

•● *Ascend to the first floor rooms.*

Blue Breakfast Room. This was remodelled for Lady Waldegrave as a 'Turkish boudoir' in 1858.

The lower part of the fireplace is the work of *Robinson*, 1748, who began the conversion of Strawberry Hill until he was demoted, by Walpole, to Clerk of Works.

Armoury or **Library Anteroom**. Here were displayed Walpole's collection of suits of armour.

Library. Work here by *Chute* includes bookcases based on drawings of the doors of the screen in Old St Paul's Cathedral and the chimney-piece inspired by John of Eltham's tomb in Westminster Abbey.

Walpole himself designed the ceiling, based on Jacobean work.

Star Chamber. This was completed in 1754. The window was recently rebuilt by *Richardson*.

Holbein Chamber. Holbein's drawings in the royal collection at Windsor were traced for Walpole and originally hung on the walls of this room, hence its name.

Bentley completed the chamber in 1758 as a guest room. The screen's inspiration was the choir gate of Rouen Cathedral.

Rouen's high altar supplied part of the design of the chimney-piece, and Archbishop Wareham's tomb in Canterbury Cathedral was copied for another section.

The ceiling is a replica of that in the Queen's Dressing Room in the State Apartments at Windsor Castle.

Long Gallery. Interior work was executed jointly by *Chute* and *Pitt* in 1763.

The ceiling vault is a copy of the fan vaulted aisles of the Henry VII Chapel at Westminster Abbey.

St Alban's Abbey's north door provided the design of the door. It has been renewed. Canopies and niches reproduce part of Archbishop Bouchier's tomb in Canterbury Cathedral.

Chapel or **Cabinet**. Completed by *Chute* in 1763, this was originally a cabinet but has since been consecrated.

Its ceiling vault is based on York Minster's Chapter House.

Round Room. The ceiling design reproduces the tracery of Old St Paul's rose window.

Panelling in the bay window was inspired by Eleanor of Castile's tomb in Westminster Abbey.

The fireplace, by *Adam*, was based on Edward the Confessor's shrine at Westminster but 'improved' according to Walpole.

Visitors are generally conducted through the 19C wing, added by Lady Waldegrave.

Immediately south of the porter's lodge is the Chapel in the Wood. This was designed by *Chute* in 1772 but the work was executed by *Gayfere* in 1774.

● Exit from Strawberry Hill. Cross the road and take bus 33 to Richmond Station (BR), District Line.